Mind Hacking for Rebels

Advance Praise for
Mind Hacking for Rebels

Wow, what a book! Amazing. I read *Mind Hacking for Rebels* to my friend—about the subconscious—which Karin explains so well this book. Her reaction was, "Oh my gosh, why don't we learn this in school? This is very important to understand." I love the layout of the book and the exercises. It has given me so many insights. You love all the wisdom Karin shares.

—Marika Jonmar

I didn't want to put down *Mind Hacking for Rebels*. I would have liked to have this book a long time ago. A nugget of gold in my bookshelf. It gets five stars out of five. With Karin's mind hacks, I am able to work with myself to become a better version of myself in all areas of my life. The book is like a therapist to carry through life. It's a real gem!

—Petra Svensson

I appreciate Karin for changing my life. I have stuck with the many good habits she taught me, and I feel much better. It feels wonderful. I read pieces of *Mind Hacking for Rebels* every night.

—Susanne Broberg

Mind Hacking for Rebels is so straightforward. I have finally received an answer as to why I react the way I do in certain situations. I have started applying some of the tips, and they work surprisingly well. Some of my counterproductive patterns have already begun to change. In fact, it doesn't have to be that difficult to create change.

—Johan Gustafsson

Karin's hacks stick! They cannot be praised enough and should be used in school. The book is pure and simple general education about how we operate and how we lead ourselves forward. Life knowledge for new times!

—**Jana Dusenberg**

Mind Hacking for Rebels is an extremely good book! Indispensable in life. Lucky for us that Karin decided to write it. Thanks!

—**Stefan Wimark**

I read half of *Mind Hacking for Rebels* in one weekend, and I just sucked everything in. It's worth gold to me, my precious gold nugget! Very easy to understand . . . an inspiring book. I'm so glad Karin wrote it so many can get your help and knowledge.

—**Susanne Brober**

A superb "healing book," in my opinion. Programming and soulfulness in one.

—**Lotta Borgsten**

Mind Hacking for Rebels is now constantly next to my bed, a bit like an encyclopedia. Every night I find something new and interesting. A jewel, as someone wrote. Thanks!

—**Jenny Melin**

I'm currently reading *Mind Hacking for Rebels*. There are many AHA-moments and tears. Just love it!

—**Janet Vendel**

Mind Hacking for Rebels is the most important book I have read. I'm devouring it. I need it. I'm so glad Karin wrote it.

—**Eva Inngul**

MIND
HACKING
FOR REBELS

OR FOR YOU WHO WANT TO BECOME ONE

A Practical Guide to
Power and Freedom

KARIN TYDÉN

NEW YORK

LONDON • NASHVILLE • MELBOURNE • VANCOUVER

Mind Hacking for Rebels

A Practical Guide to Power and Freedom

Published in New York, New York, by Morgan James Publishing. Morgan James is a trademark of Morgan James, LLC. www.MorganJamesPublishing.com

Morgan James BOGO™

A **FREE** ebook edition is available for you or a friend with the purchase of this print book.

CLEARLY SIGN YOUR NAME ABOVE

Instructions to claim your free ebook edition:
1. Visit MorganJamesBOGO.com
2. Sign your name CLEARLY in the space above
3. Complete the form and submit a photo of this entire page
4. You or your friend can download the ebook to your preferred device

ISBN 9781631955266 paperback
ISBN 9781631955273 ebook
Library of Congress Control Number:
2021931763

Cover & Interior Design by:
Christopher Kirk
www.GFSstudio.com

Morgan James is a proud partner of Habitat for Humanity Peninsula and Greater Williamsburg. Partners in building since 2006.

Get involved today! Visit
MorganJamesPublishing.com/giving-back

CONTENTS

ACKNOWLEDGMENTS

To my special friends—Teresia, Anette, and Nina—who have been the three pillars in my life this year, supporting me to make this book happen. To the clients that have relentlessly encouraged me to write the book, thank you.

Thank you to my publisher, Jim Howard, at Morgan James Publishing for believing that this book should be in everyone's hand. And to my editor, Cortney Donelson, for elevating the book one more step.

It shall be.

ABOUT ME

I am an adventurer and like to go far out to the outer edges. Sometimes, I have been so far out that I wondered if I would ever find my way back again.

I was born into a religious family with strict rules where the word of God was law. My dad, whom I loved above everyone else, was a narcissist. At times, he was amazing and took me on breathtaking adventures.

We climbed in the mountains and swam in the sea under heavy rain and rumbling thunder. We slalom skied behind the car in white snowy landscapes and looked for treasures in hard-to-reach caves. He taught me about nature, taking care of sick animals, building huts, and shooting with a bow and a rifle. He taught me about space and how to dance the Viennese waltz. He taught me proper etiquette and to appreciate the beautiful things in life.

When dad was unbalanced, he became moody and mean. Mom was a shadow— emotionally closed off and hard to reach but also someone who tried her best to be a good mother. But she was without significance in the patriarchal religion. I have suffered abuse, been beaten, alienated, publicly punished and humiliated, and both forced and oppressed, all to make me a better person.

The day I turned eighteen, I took my suitcase and left my old life behind. I did a total reboot, a *reset*. Without family, support, money, or experience of the outside world, I began to build my own life. I created a good life, one in which I was successful in most things. I had well-paying and exciting jobs in TV, marketing, branding, and public relations, mostly good boyfriends, cool friends, and a crazy drive to maximize life.

At age thirty-five, everything caught up with me. Old unprocessed experiences and programming wreaked havoc in me, and I decided to do a *reset*. This restart was going to be tough because I had to face everything I had hidden in my subconscious. The journey took twenty years. Today, I stand strong and free. I own my POWER and FREEDOM. Of course, I can still doubt myself sometimes, make mistakes, feel weak, and think that I should be better, smarter, faster, kinder . . . but on the whole, I feel like a good person, that I am enough. It's a great feeling!

My dad was called "The Thousandth" at his work. He loved to take apart things to see the mechanics behind them and then manufacture and replace the parts that didn't work. I'm the same when it comes to personal development. I love to explore and understand how we humans work. I travel through time and space, to explore "reality" and replace the parts that don't work. I am an adventurer and like to travel to the outer edges. Sometimes, I have traveled so far that I have wondered if I would ever find my way back again. From childhood wounds, career stress, depression, self-hatred, confusion, sadness, and desperation, I have created a brilliant way of coaching.

Today, I work as a Mind Hacker and love to change people's reality. I help people all over the world to clear mental, emotional, and spiritual obstacles to help them find their POWER and create their FREEDOM. To avoid taking the long route, like I had to do, I have developed a way of working with hypnosis, which allows me to create major changes in a person's life in just a few sessions. With my highly sensitive ability, I can take in tons of information about a person, sense the smallest ripple in their energy, find the deepest problems, and solve them. I have the ability to understand the mechanics of people's thoughts, feelings, and behaviors, to access the programming that created the problem, and to quickly create new thoughts, feelings, and behaviors. The abuse, punishments, and humiliation of my childhood have helped me become resourceful, given me the courage to venture into the dark and hard stuff with my clients, and to find a way out.

With this book I want to inspire you to become a rebel and own your POWER and FREEDOM!

ABOUT THE BOOK

I rebel; therefore, I exist.
—Albert Camus[1]

To be a rebel is to create your own identity, to challenge, to face the truth, to make your own choices, to stand up for yourself, to say what you think and how you feel, to believe in yourself and your ability, to not care about what others think, and to do what you want and not what is expected of you. To become a leader in your own life. I intend to inspire more people to become rebels.

I'm a rebel. When I was eighteen, I left my family, my friends, and my home behind me and took on life headfirst. I had almost no experience with the outside world, no money, no education, and no idea what direction I should take. I was alone. Luckily, I didn't know what a tough trip it would be at times; otherwise, I might not have dared to start my adventure.

This book has come about based on a wish that I had these Jedi Mind Tricks[2] when I started my personal growth journey so that it had been both easier and

---

1   Albert Camus (Nov 07, 1913–Jan 04, 1960) was one of the twentieth century's most famous philosophers and a Nobel laureate in Literature at the age of forty-four, the second youngest ever.
2   Jedi—a member of an order of knights in the *Star Wars* movies. The Jedi Knights believed in an invisible universal energy, called The Force—also known as the life force—the good side,

gone faster. I want to help you become a rebel. It may not mean leaving everything behind, but rather leaving what is no longer useful to you—old structures, limitations, and fears. I want you to own your own POWER and FREEDOM to create your own future.

I don't claim to hold any absolute truth, but in my job as a Mind Hacker and coach, I've met thousands of people. In these meetings, I have begun to understand patterns of how our problems, limitations, barriers, and fears arise and what is needed to create change, let go, and begin to heal. There are many different approaches among coaches, therapists, philosophers, and researchers on how to look at things. I have chosen to highlight the aspects that appeal to me the most and the tools that have created quick and profound results for my clients.

I have deliberately avoided filling the book with references to scientific studies and citations. I have simplified my reasoning to create an easily accessible book, one that quickly gets to the heart of the matter. I make no claims, offer any diagnoses, or promise to cure you. I hope you will change your way of looking at yourself and life. If I can help you experience a tenth of what I have learned, I will be very happy.

The book mixes facts, founded in scientific studies, with reflections and observations from thousands of hours with clients around the world. I offer some of my best tips, the most important insights, and the most effective #mindhacks[3] that have crossed my path. If you are a fact junkie, I recommend you use Google to search for more information on the web. At the end of the book, you will find a list of resources that I think are worth reading.

DISCLAIMER

Although many of the book's #mindhacks have scientific studies that back them, and thousands of people have used them to make major changes in their lives, I can't guarantee any results. It relies heavily on your own commitment and your will to change. Nor can I take responsibility for interpretations and choices you make in connection with the book and its hacks. If you have a

---

the light side. The Jedi Knights used this power to maintain peace and justice in the galaxy.
3   Hacks—mind hacking is all about finding the most effective ways to optimize your mindset. Hacks are simple, quick tips on how to do this in practice.

diagnosis or are mentally unwell, I recommend you contact your health care provider for further assistance.

APPROACH

Here are some tips on how to get the most out of the book and yourself.

1. **Read for insights, not information.** Insights are rare and precious, unlike information that is just data. An insight is a discovery of something that has previously been hidden and creates a new perspective about ourselves and the world. We often have to rethink what we previously thought and knew. Therefore, let what you read sink in. Insights may not come immediately. The penny may drop several weeks later, while you're sitting in the car on your way to work or standing in the shower. Be patient, your insights will come when you are ready.

2. **Don't renovate the entire house at the same time.** If you read the book in one sitting, it can feel overwhelming with all the hacks. Follow the principle: "Don't renovate the whole house at the same time." Pick out a few #mindhacks and repeat them until they work. You can also select specific parts of your life that you want to work on. Small renovations allow you to grow in your everyday life.

3. **Do it your own way.** There are principles for the human mind and how it works. If you understand the mechanisms behind your programming and how they work, you can play with the rules and find your unique superpowers. See the hacks as possible ways to prosper, but let your process be personal.

4. **See your development as an adventure, not a task.** The content of the book is not a task you should tick off your list or have the correct answer to. Explore. Have an open mind. Don't stress about it. The book doesn't need to be read from cover to cover unless you absolutely want to. Read a chapter now and then. Have a Yoda Moment[4]. Try the hacks. Be curious!

---

4 Yoda—a character in the *Star Wars* movies. Legendary Jedi Master and leader of the Jedi Order's Supreme Council. Extremely wise and stronger than most in his contact with "The Force." Yoda lived to be 900 years old.

HOW SOON CAN I SEE THE RESULTS?

Your reward will depend on the effort you put in. You need to keep practicing and have some patience. Most people notice that the results grow over time. Be aware, changes tend to sneak up on you. Suddenly you discover that you are no longer afraid, that you are happier, or that you react differently in a certain situation. A good tip is to keep a journal where you write down every little change you notice. It's really fun to be able to go back and see how much you have progressed.

Join the Mind Hacking Movement!

Stay in Touch

www.karintyden.se

TO BECOME A REBEL

Mind Hacking is about finding the most effective ways
to optimize your mindset.

Movie scene: An abandoned old hotel room with flaking wallpaper. A man sits reclined in a leather armchair. He's wearing sunglasses and a black leather trench coat. Opposite him is a young computer programmer. Thunder is rolling in the background.

"What truth?" asks Neo, the computer programmer.

The man called Morpheus leans in. "That you are a slave, Neo. Like everyone else, you were born into bondage. Born into a prison you cannot smell or taste or touch. A prison . . . for your mind. Unfortunately, no one can be told what The Matrix is; you have to see it for yourself." (From the movie, *The Matrix*, 1999)[5]

---

5 Lana and Lilly Wachowski, dirs. *The Matrix*. Burbank, CA: Warner Brothers and Village Roadshow Pictures, 1999.

Gradually, Neo understands that he has lived in a simulated reality, that The Matrix is a data code, and that with his powerful mind, he can bypass the rules of the simulated reality The Matrix has created. Neo joins the rebels. He learns how The Matrix works and how to stretch the physical laws that exist in the reality most people live in and how to get superpowers. The goal is freedom from slavery.

Some interpret the prison in the form of the simulated reality in the movie *The Matrix* as the world and society we live in; others draw parallels to our own mental prisons. No matter what, our thought loops keep us trapped in a prison with invisible walls, where we are convinced that our reality is the only true one and that it cannot be changed. But just like in *The Matrix,* we can hack the code, play with the rules, and get superpowers.

WHAT IS MIND HACKING?

The term *hacker* originated in the computer programming subcultures of the 1960s. It was used to describe people who tackled difficult problems in the spirit of playful exploration and who had difficulties with authorities who didn't deserve their power. They were rebels. Although the hackers' methods and intentions varied, many of them seemed to have a unique ethos—a combination of a strong commitment, a desire for independence and freedom, and a desire to collaborate and create together.

Over time, the term "hacking" has been given a wider interpretation, and today, there is biohacking, consciousness hacking, flow hacking, mind hacking, brain hacking, neurohacking, and life hacking, to name a few examples.

It is said that the word *hacking* originated in 1955 when it was used by MIT to describe an unusual solution to a complex problem. Common for all kinds of hacking, regardless of type, is that you try to find the most effective ways to optimize the human experience. An important theme for all hackers is *self-responsibility*. Hackers believe we can no longer rely on external authorities to take care of us. By combining information that is available, individual experimentation, and open collaboration, we can take responsibility for our own development and create the life we want to have.

Mind Hacking involves using unconventional and sometimes new techniques to gain access to the mechanisms inside the human mind. Mind Hacking is focused on finding the most effective ways to optimize your mindset. To change your thoughts, feelings, experiences, interpretations, and actions in the fastest and most effective way so that you can find your own POWER and FREEDOM. To become who you want to be, to create the life you want, you need to take responsibility for your own process. You need to become a hacker. A rebel.

> *Hacker:* "A person who enjoys learning the details of programming systems and how to stretch their capabilities, as opposed to most users who prefer to learn only the minimum necessary."
>
> —The Hacker's Dictionary

HOW DO I BECOME A REBEL?

Albert Camus, one of the most talked about philosophers and Nobel laureates in literature of the twentieth century said, "I rebel; therefore, I exist." To be a rebel is to create your own identity, to question, to form your own opinion, to stand up for yourself, to make your own choices, to dare to say what you think and feel, to not care about what others think, to do what you want and not what is expected of you, and to become a leader in your own life. It is essentially what we often define as having good self-confidence and a strong self-esteem.

Anyone can become a rebel. You just have to decide that you want to and then take one step at a time. Let the hacker's three principles inspire you.

Principle #1. Hacking is free and belongs to everyone.
You are free to use, modify and share these #mindhacks with others. Become a pioneer and share what you learn. Become a positive role model that others can follow.

Principle #2. Hacking is experimental (and you are the experiment).
Test, adjust, retest, fail, retest, re-evaluate, retest . . . I encourage curiosity. You need to be curious and a little brave because sometimes, you have to step far outside your comfort zone. You need to be a rebel because sometimes you have to break the rules.

Principle #3. Hacking means becoming a master.
A true hacker can be defined by a will to conquer a small part of the world, whether that is to know all of the songs by The Beatles in chronological order, own the world's largest collection of sneakers, or hold the highest possible score in Guitar Hero III. A hacker wants to make the impossible possible. To become a champion of your own mind, you need to persevere and practice, practice, practice.

It's time to dive into your own Matrix!

CHAPTER 1 IN 60 SECONDS

- When you hack the code of your own matrix, you can play with the rules and get superpowers.
- Mind Hacking is understanding the mechanisms inside the human mind and finding the most effective ways to optimize your mindset.
- For all hackers, the common theme is your own responsibility, through which you can create your own POWER and FREEDOM.
- To be a rebel is to create your own identity and become a leader in your own life.
- Hacking is free and belongs to everyone. In hacking you are the experiment. A hacker wants to make the impossible possible.

THE MATRIX

The matrix is the collection of programs that control your thoughts, emotions, and behaviors. Your beliefs are the rules of the game.

I n order to change your matrix, you first need to understand what the matrix is and how it works. The matrix is a code, a programming. If you think, feel, and act in a way that doesn't feel good to you, there is nothing wrong with you. It's your matrix that's incorrectly programmed.

WHAT IS THE MATRIX?

The matrix is the collection of programs that control our thoughts, feelings, and behaviors. The matrix is in our subconscious mind and contains all of the code we have been programmed with since birth. The subconscious is like a large database. Here, all our experiences, beliefs, memories, and skills are stored: everything we have learned and everything our surroundings have programmed us with; how we should act to be loved, accepted, and safe; how to avoid pain; what is right and wrong; and what we are allowed, or not, to think, feel, and do. It tells us what is possible and what isn't. What we can or cannot do. Our self-value, or lack thereof. The matrix is a system of beliefs, a number of "truths," or convictions, about ourselves and our world, the possibilities and limitations we have. This is a fantastic survival mechanism created by nature. A child must quickly learn to understand his or her surroundings and all its rules to be loved, accepted, understood, and safe. Based on all the stored experiences, the child then understands how a certain behavior leads to security and access to the community. We can have both positive/expanding and negative/limiting programming in our subconscious minds. All of this stored information forms our operating system, our matrix, which directs us every day to survive, feel good, and function in our society. Most of what we think, feel, and do is controlled by this operating system.

HOW DOES THE MATRIX WORK?

Since the time we were children, we have formed different beliefs about ourselves and life. We have also created countless strategies to succeed in life. When our subconscious accepted something as a truth, it became our reality. We live according to these "truths" all our lives, whether good or bad, true or not. Our beliefs and strategies become our rules. By the age of thirty-five, 95 percent of us have a set of beliefs, attitudes, memorized behaviors, and emotional reactions that work just like computer programs. The subconscious database where all information is stored is the computer that runs all the programs. Let me give you an example.

You have a manager who, when conflicts arise, shies away and lets the employees solve the problems themselves. You are angry with your boss and think he's not taking his responsibility. One possible explanation for shying away during conflicts could be that, as a child, he often saw his parents fighting, something he couldn't control or solve. The fighting escalated; he became scared and pulled away to his room. Your boss learned, as a child, how to deal with fear and powerlessness by hiding from what is causing these feelings. The strategy your boss chose as a child is then automatically used during the rest of his life, unless he consciously chooses another action or strategy. Each time your boss notices that a conflict is on the way, his subconscious programming, the matrix, is activated in the same way. Your boss experiences the same feelings as when he was a little boy—fear and powerlessness—and then he chooses the same strategy as he did then: to shy away to his room.

Neuroscientists have found that our subconscious, with all our programming, controls about 95 percent of our daily behaviors. This means that the subconscious can decide for us, long before we make a conscious decision. Therefore, we can sometimes feel as if something within us has "hijacked" us and taken over. When a conflict arises, your boss is no longer an adult. He has been hijacked by his subconscious program, and he responds in the exact same way as he did when he was a child. The subconscious does not evaluate whether the program is good or bad; it only runs the program that has been installed until we change the program. If we are unlucky and our programming has been wrong from the start, the subconscious can run destructive programs that are not good for us. There is nothing wrong with the computer. It just runs the program that has been installed. Therefore, do not be harsh or criticize yourself; there is nothing wrong with you. It's the programming that is wrong. That is what you will learn to change.

FIVE PERCENT AGAINST NINETY-FIVE

Imagine you're riding a giant elephant. If you have trained the elephant well, you can steer it where you want it to go. But if you have an elephant that wants to go in a different direction, there is not much you can do. Our subconscious is like the elephant. It can either be controlled by the driver, our conscious mind, or it can go its own way and step on whatever gets in its way.

The conscious part of the brain, our modern brain, and the youngest part of our evolutionary development, is logical and analytical. The prefrontal cortex, a part of the brain's frontal lobe, is our command center and will help us set direction and goals, process information, plan, focus, show good judgment, solve problems, make conscious choices, and propel us forward. The subconscious will then automate everything we do, making life easier for us. Using our conscious mind, we have the opportunity to see the various active programs, and we can stop them at any time. But this is where the problem arises. We often overestimate the power of the conscious mind. It is just an add-on in our evolution and can only handle what it focuses on, which isn't that much. According to neuroscientists, the conscious mind is active for about 5 percent of the day. The rest, an astounding 95 percent, is taken care of by the subconscious, which controls almost everything we do. According to neuroscientist Joe Dispenza, the conscious mind can only handle about 2,000 bits of information per second, while the subconscious mind can handle 400 billion bits of information per second.[6] Developmental biologist Bruce Lipton describes the subconscious mind as a million times stronger than the conscious mind, and it makes over a thousand times more decisions each day than the conscious mind. The subconscious can process a lot of information in a short time and therefore, makes the most decisions.

So, in many everyday situations, you only focus on a few things that are happening, the subconscious takes care of the rest, and you have no idea what program is running. If it then runs a subconscious program that is not in your favor—and that you don't even notice—it can sabotage you, and you'll have no idea why things aren't going your way. If your conscious mind has an intention and wants to go in one direction, but your subconscious has a completely different program and wants to go in another direction, your subconscious will win over the conscious mind almost every time.

Let's look at an example. You're single and at a party. Suddenly, your Prince Charming is standing in front of you. He's smiling at you. The conscious part of your brain (if still functioning) thinks: he is smiling at me. I'm going to go ahead and say hello. I actually want to meet a nice guy and start a family. However, your subconscious mind might have a completely different idea. You have been through a few tough relationships, and the subconscious mind carefully keeps track of everything that indicates relationships can be dangerous, that you can be hurt. Instead of going ahead and saying hello, the subconscious takes over and sends you to the buffet at the other end of the room. There, you have some cheese and some wine and wonder what is wrong with you.

THE DOWNLOAD PERIOD

We can compare birth to landing on a whole new planet as an adult, where we quickly must understand how to survive. We have an instinct to survive and belong. Not belonging is the most dangerous social mistake for a human being.

---

6   Arntz, William, et. al. *What the Bleep Do We Know!?*. Production split by Mr. X Inc. (Toronto, Canada), Lost Boys Studios (Vancouver, Canada), and Atomic Visual Effects (Cape Town, South Africa), 2004.

An animal that is excluded from the flock is in grave danger. A child who is excluded from the family or the community faces certain death. We know this deep within us, whether it is a genetic or a social memory. Being different from our family or tribe is dangerous and can lead to rejection, abandonment, or exclusion from the group.

Nature has therefore designed it so that 80 percent of brain development occurs between birth and three years of age, and during the first six to seven years of our life, we are extremely open to learning. We can call this the download period. We observe everything. We see how our parents and other adults behave and how they relate to themselves, others, and life. We learn what love looks like. We learn what is possible. We learn how to act to be loved, accepted, safe, and how to avoid pain at a remarkable speed. We simply download all the rules of the game. It's a pure survival mechanism.

One of our most basic survival strategies is to become as similar as possible to our caretakers. There are special neurons, mirror neurons, which allow us to mirror and imitate them. We imitate their behavior, which gives us positive attention. "Look, Lisa is smiling back. Isn't she cute?" The disadvantage of being so open to learning is that we are completely uncritical. If Mom screams when she sees a spider, spiders become dangerous. If, on the other hand, Mom is an enthusiastic spider scientist, spiders will be interesting. As young children we do not argue about whether spiders are dangerous or interesting.

The conscious part of us that is logical, analytical, and values the information we let in— where we can interpret, understand, and draw the right conclusions about people, things and situations—is not fully developed until we are around twenty-five years old. Instead, as children, we let most things in without reflecting on whether they are good or bad, and then all this information is stored in the subconscious. Our foundation is complete and our deepest beliefs are already in place at the age of six or seven. If Dad asked you, "How many times have I told you . . ." your default setting may end up being "I'm stupid. I can't do it" when you've heard it enough times. If you were criticized as a child when you did things, you won't try anything new. If your parents often showed you what was right and wrong, you became passive and took no initiative, you waited until you were told to do something. Our beliefs often arise because something has been repeated many times.

However, it's important to emphasize that not all of our programming is done while we are children. We have experiences and encounter situations and people that affect us even as teenagers and adults.

HOW OUR PROGRAMS ARE INSTALLED

There are several things that can affect our programming. Some of the most important ones are:

- Biological preprogramming
- How we are brought up and treated
- The role models we have around us
- Our experiences and our interpretations of what happens
- The brain misdirects
- The brain's focus on survival and protection
- The brain's focus on energy saving

Biological Pre-Programming

We have hundreds of biological, pre-programmed survival mechanisms. An example is babies who express fear and get upset when left alone or are surprised by a stranger. Babies also have a strong pre-programming to explore when they feel safe. Another example is our craving for sweet, salt, and fat. These flavors were not always available to our ancestors, so our bodies are pre-programmed to look for them, feel a craving for them when they are available, and eat them when we find them. Thousands of years ago, this was a fantastic feature; it ensured our survival. Today, when food is available twenty-four hours a day, it is not as good. Food producers know what our biology is attracted to. To sell more, they fill processed foods with sugar, salt, and fat in a perfect mix.

Upbringing and Treatment

Based on how we are nurtured and treated by our surroundings, our beliefs and strategies are created and become more numerous and stronger until they fully control our lives. The old Jesuits (a male Catholic order that abides by the Pope) understood this in the sixteenth century when they said, "Give me the child for the first seven years, and I will give you the man." What adults say about us, say to us, and how they treat us is important. What adults don't say also plays a big role. If they omit praise, encouragement, and understanding or just focus on what we do wrong, we can grow up with a sense that we are not valuable or capable or have a fear of making mistakes and failing. Usually, our parents and other adults mean well; they just want us to succeed. They want us to fit in so things will go well for us. To develop a good self-esteem, a child needs to be treated as a valuable person whose needs are important.

Our Role Models

Good role models are important when it comes to building sound beliefs and strategies. When we are young, we take in everything we see and hear from others, and that becomes our truth. It's only when we're adults that we can create our own truth. What authorities say and how they behave set examples of how things should work or be done. How adults behave is often what we learn to do ourselves in adulthood. If we are aware, we can change these programs. If your parents didn't show emotions often and rarely said "I love you," as an adult, you can consciously decide that you should be loving and say "I love you" as often as you can to your children or partner. But there is a risk that you unknowingly adopt the style of your parents and do the same to your children or your partner.

Our Experiences and Interpretations

Experiences that may seem small in the rear-view mirror are often a big deal from a child's perspective. Getting a scolding, experiencing a divorce, changing schools, getting a sibling, getting lost in the store, or falling of a horse can create programming in us, which, later in life, limits us. Positive experiences also affect us and can make us feel safe, strong, and important. The imprints that are made are often related to how we interpret what has happened.

Our young brain is driven by figuring things out and learning how everything works. Toddlers are like little scientists. They observe, experiment, and draw conclusions. "If I cry, I'll be comforted." "If I throw my pacifier, it will come back." We observe the world and give meaning to what is happening. Every conclusion we make is added to our stock of beliefs. Things that happen, without anyone really making a mistake or having a bad intention, can be negatively interpreted by a child. Let me give you an example.

CLIENT STORY

Sharing the Spotlight

Madeleine wanted help with her low self-esteem, which caused her to give others priority and rarely stand up for herself and her needs. During the session, we found that self-esteem had begun to falter at age four when her little sister was born. Suddenly, she was no longer the center of attention. The spotlight was split. Madeleine felt the baby was getting more attention and that she was no longer as important. Everyone cuddled and played with the baby, while she was told that she should be a good big sister. Madeleine believed that more was required of her, while her little sister had it easier. Her self-esteem took a hit. A four-year-old may not understand that she is just as important but that the baby needs more attention in the beginning because of her helplessness. She may not have understood that you cannot expect the same things of a newborn as you can of a four-year-old. This may be the first seed of low self-esteem. The parents haven't consciously overlooked Madeleine, but it is Madeleine's own interpretation of the situation that has created her belief that she is not as important. When Madeleine realized that her interpretation didn't actually match reality, she could replace it with a more positive one. She began to see her own worth and what she contributed. As a result, Madeleine began to stand up for herself and her self-esteem was strengthened.

An event that is misinterpreted and impairs the self-esteem can then be added to other situations where you have felt overlooked or less important—some true and some based on your own interpretation. Finally, the belief is cemented and saved as your default mode. Your brain loves to automate to save energy and make it easy. After this, the risk becomes much greater that your autopilot interprets different events in your adult life in exactly the same way as when you were a child: you are not good enough; you are not important. You start to think that others are better and know more. You begin to make decisions and act on the basis of your belief that you are not important. You attract people and situations that confirm what you already know—you are not important. You don't stand up for yourself or your needs. You're attracted to people who don't respect you. The downward spiral continues.

It's important to understand that we don't have to experience what we would define as a major trauma in order for us to experience fears, anxieties, insecurities, or lack of self-esteem and self-confidence. When we are children and our brains and nervous system are still developing, we can develop a sense of insecurity when we are left at Kindergarten, when mom or dad get annoyed when we do something wrong, or when we are teased in school. This can make us feel compelled to pay extra attention to our surroundings, and we have, therefore, become accustomed to being on constant alert. The nervous system doesn't allow us to relax because then something bad can happen . . . because it did so during our childhood. The inner turmoil as an adult is the consequence of having been prepared for emergency ever since we were small.

When the Brain Misdirects

One variation of interpretation is when the brain misdirects, which I encounter a lot in my work as a coach. In situations when something happens, the brain takes a snapshot of its surroundings and can then link the various components of the image with, for example, danger, simply to avoid danger in the future. A good example of this transpired during a session I had with a man who came to me because of his constant worrying. What is interesting is that we not only found the cause of his concern but also his sensitivity to gluten. When he was a young student at university, he was often stressed about assignments, exams, and deadlines. Every morning, when he was hurrying to a lecture, he biked past a bakery to buy buns to have as an extra energy supply during the day. The brain and immune system linked buns with stress and danger, and therefore, alerted him each time he ate the buns. When his subconscious realized that the stress didn't come from eating the buns but from completely different things, his gluten sensitivity disappeared.

Another interesting example was a woman who was afraid of dogs, even though she could not remember having ever experienced an unpleasant dog encounter. We found an experience when she, as a two- or three-year-old, sat on the floor and played. Her mother dropped something in the kitchen, and it made a lot of noise. The little girl jumped in fear, her brain took a snapshot of the surroundings, and at that moment, a dog on the TV. The brain linked the fear and shock to the dog, and her fear of dogs became a fact.

We can also misinterpret what it is that makes us feel good or bad. A common example is when we think our partner makes us feel a certain way, whether it is happiness or dissatisfaction. Instead of realizing that there can be other reasons for how we feel, such as our internal programming and thought patterns, we make it easy for ourselves by blaming our environment or those around us. We direct all our attention to what is happening outside us and thus, also direct all our energy there.

Survival and Protection

Since your brain wants to create security and make sure you survive, it doesn't like to do something new, difficult, scary, dangerous, or inconvenient. It will scan for anything negative, so you don't miss anything that could threaten your security or survival. Therefore, your brain doesn't like to go outside its comfort zone. Instead, it likes everything that is familiar, things it recognizes, because that creates a sense of security and control. So when we, as children, have found strategies that guarantee us love and security, we prefer not to change them. Even if the strategies are not good for us in the long run and prevent us from being everything we want to be.

In addition, our conscious and subconscious mind can have different opinions about what is best for us. It is quite common for there to be a conflict between the wishes and strategies of the conscious and those of the subconscious. For example, if you weigh too much and want to lose weight, your conscious mind probably knows that's a great idea. The subconscious mind might have a completely differ-ent view. If your subconscious thinks old emotional pain will come to the surface if you stop eating as much, then the subconscious will say no, you should not lose weight. If your subconscious has a program installed that says *you're not worth feeling good about yourself*, the subconscious will hold onto that belief because it is "true" and say no, you should not lose weight. If there is a risk that you will fail to lose weight and experience disappointment and self-contempt, the subconscious will protect you from these feelings by saying no, you should not lose weight. If your subconscious has learned that ending relationships hurts, and if you lose weight, you will likely enter a new relationship with the risk of being hurt again, the subconscious will say no, you should not lose weight. The subconscious tries to protect you from pain. Anything new and uncertain can potentially be dan-gerous, so the subconscious thinks it's best to stay where you are. Therefore, the subconscious can choose to keep the strategy, even if you don't consciously think it is a good one.

Save Energy

There is another reason why the subconscious mind makes the most decisions in your life. Your brain wants to save energy for future needs and does so by automating and simplifying most of what you do. It is called your default mode network (DMN), or the autopilot. Your autopilot is very good to have, so you don't have to think about everything. Imagine if every time you brushed your teeth, you had to think about how to hold your toothbrush. Or how to turn on the coffee machine. Or how to open the front door. Your subconscious mind lets you do lots of things on autopilot; otherwise, you would have zero energy left in your brain.

You probably remember when you learned to drive a car. You were very aware of all the tasks you had to perform. Driving the car took all of your focus. Your conscious mind couldn't handle all the information, and there were things the instructor had to remind you about. Today, several years later, you can drive and simultaneously discuss topics with your passengers, listen to music, or sit and think about a presentation you will give at work the next day. All of a sudden, you arrive at your destination without really knowing how you got there. Your subconscious is driving while your conscious is doing something else. When something gets repetitive, it happens automatically. That's how the brain saves energy.

The subconscious mind can run a lot of programs that help us in everyday life and help the brain save energy. The problem is not that we automate but when we go on autopilot, when we should instead be in direct mode. Where we should create, relate, focus, plan, and make conscious choices. If we run on autopilot and our programming is negative, we will not think before we act, and our choices will be random or at worst, wrong. When we have automated negative thoughts about ourselves—our skills and our self-value—we devalue ourselves.

Since your brain wants to save energy, it can become quite comfortable. It takes shortcuts and selects thought patterns and behaviors it has chosen many times before. That's when you get stuck in a route. The more times you have taken that route, the harder the pattern is to break. In the end, breaking your pattern can be very difficult, even if you want to.

WHAT KINDS OF PROGRAMMING CAN WE HAVE?

There's no limit. Programming can be neutral findings and facts without any emotional connection. They can be general or specific, conscious choices or spontaneous, or negative and limiting or positive and reinforcing. They can even be inherited. Research shows that memories can be inherited biologically through chemical changes that occur in our DNA.

The most common limiting and negative programming statements I hear from my clients are:

- I'm not _____ (valuable, talented, a good person . . .)
- I don't _____ (matter, deserve, dare, know . . .)
- I can't _____ (do it, manage, make it . . .)
- I'm not _____ enough (important, smart, sweet, good, rich . . .)
- I don't have enough _____ (time, money, support, energy, friends, trust in others . . .)
- I don't want people to think I'm _____ (stupid, boring, weak, unsuccessful . . .)

- I'm _____ (powerless, boring, uninteresting, alone, stupid, disappointing, too young, too old . . .)
- No one _____ (likes me, loves me, listens, understands me, does anything . . .)
- I'm afraid to _____ (fail, get hurt, embarrass myself, get rejected . . .)
- It _____ (is impossible, is no use, never happens, always fails . . .)

If our subconscious has been programmed with experiences that makes us think we are losers, not good enough, or can't manage, these thought patterns will eventually become part of our standard program. Thoughts and feelings start to go on autopilot mode. Our inner negative voice is now a part of our default mode network. And when we think and feel that we are not good enough, that we are worthless or don't deserve nice things, then we start to act accordingly. We have created our own truth, our own mental prison.

Our subconscious minds will then:

- Run the program that works best for the situation we are in, focusing on protecting us from pain, surviving, and helping us to be loved, accepted, and safe. We can call this program The Guardian.
- Run the program that we were brought up to believe is the right one in a particular situation. We can call this program The Parent.
- Run a standard program based on the conclusions we have drawn about ourselves, our abilities, and our self-value, all based on how we have been treated. We can call this program The Identity.

THE GUARDIAN

Our programs are often coded early in our lives, when our ability to understand things and choose a sound strategy was limited. This means that our strategy can be counterproductive in adulthood and sometimes remind of a child. Let me give an example of how the Guardian can be installed and how it can protect us.

CLIENT STORY

It Hurts

When Johan stepped into my office, he seemed to be a man with good self-confidence. He was smart, nice, and good-looking. But under the surface, Johan was extremely shy when it came to women. As soon as a woman came near, he either started talking uncontrollably or he fled the situation. His biggest dream was to start a family, but this seemed impossible because he found it so difficult to approach women.

Johan had always been shy around girls, even as a young man but had hoped it would get better with age. This wasn't the case. We were able to trace the fear back to the age of eight. In his class, there was a cute girl—Jenny. She was swarmed by all the guys and Johan didn't think he had a chance. But somewhere inside, he didn't want to miss his opportunity, so he mustered his courage for a whole semester and then finally went ahead and asked her on a date. She turned him down!

During our session, Johan experienced the same shock his nervous system went through as an eight-year-old, the shock of being rejected. He experienced a pain deep inside his chest and felt powerlessness from not knowing how to deal with it. Johan's brain took a snapshot of the situation and quickly con- cluded that girls are dangerous, you can be rejected, and you can't control the pain. The Guardian began to do its job. The strategy chosen by The Guardian was to make sure that Johan talked incoherently or fled the field when a girl approached. The program ran every time he met a girl, whether when he was eight or forty-two years old. The Guardian minimizes the risk of any girl becoming interested. Either the girl thinks that Johan is weird, or she watches him disappear. In this way, Johan avoids the risk of being rejected. No rejection = no pain. There is a logic to it, don't you think?

Why do we continue using these negative—and sometimes childish—strategies into adulthood? Well, because beliefs and strategies have no expiration date. They can be kept permanently in the subconscious. The voices of criticism, doubt, fear, guilt, or worry, which you hear inside your head, are old beliefs still doing their jobs. Every belief and strategy was created at a time when there was a good reason to believe that your interpretation was correct or that this strategy was the best one—or the only available one. Once installed, it will operate forever, even if the environment or circumstances change. The subconscious thinks the strategy works; and therefore, sees no reason to replace it. After some time, the strategy becomes so integrated within us that we hardly notice it anymore. We have created a strategy that has become a habit. The longer The Guardian has worked for us, the better it will be at its job. Every time we are triggered by someone or something that can affect us negatively, it pops up and takes control. There's even a name for it: Sudden Reaction Syndrome. Someone pushes our buttons and we respond.

But this is also where a new problem arises. In Johan's case, there was a price for not being able to approach girls: loneliness, which also creates pain. So why does the subconscious prefer the pain of being alone rather than the pain of being rejected? One possible explanation is that our subconscious ranks the pain intensity, and in the case of Johan, the acute pain of being rejected was worse than the low-intensity grinding pain of being alone. I think everyone is different, but after a few thousand clients, I can definitely see a pattern. The vast majority choose the more low-key grinding pain rather than the acute high-intensity pain. It is only when the low-key grinding pain has grown so big that we can't stand it that we do something about it.

I think it's a bit like getting chafed feet. You are standing there in your fancy shoes, and they chafe your heels just a little bit, but you endure it because you look so nice in your shoes. You keep the shoes on and think it won't get any worse. A few hours later, you have painful blisters, and it hurts like crazy. This is when it becomes urgently important to change shoes.

Over time, our subconscious has learned what is positive and makes us feel good and what is painful and makes us feel bad. For the sake of our wellbeing, The Guardian protects us by creating strategies to avoid negative and painful experiences. Don't be angry with yourself for sometimes thinking, feeling, or acting counterproductively. Understand that your Guardian has only tried to help you survive physically, mentally, emotionally, and spiritually, although the strategy that worked as a child may not work as well as an adult.

THE PARENT

Our parents and other adult authorities have shown us how to handle different situations through the way they acted in similar situations. From our surroundings, we also learn what is socially accepted, normal, and appropriate. When we then face different situations in life, the subconscious picks up the strategies we have already learned and activates them, whether they are productive or not.

You have probably heard the phrase "children don't do what you tell them to do; they do what you do." This is truer than you think. If Mom or Dad have avoided standing up for themselves, the child learns to keep quiet, never argue, prioritize others first, and not express their own opinions, feelings, and needs. It's quite often that I work with clients who have never learned how to stand up for themselves, express their needs, trust themselves, or like themselves. No one has shown them how. Parents need to show their children how to handle different emotions and situations by being their role models.

THE IDENTITY

Our experiences in life have created beliefs about our own abilities and self-value. How our parents, other adults, family members, and friends treated us as children has created a standard program around who we are and what we can do. According to psychology professor Daniel Gilbert, you are in your standard mode, your autopilot, 46.9 percent of the time. And it's totally fine when you brush your teeth, put on your pants, or drink a cup of coffee but not when you think negative thoughts about yourself. Because if your default attitude about yourself, your abilities, and your self-value is negative, you will not feel good in the long run, and you won't reach your goals.

CLIENT STORY

I'm Not as Good

Susanne was never satisfied with her efforts at work. She thought everyone else was better, smarter, and more knowledgeable than her. Susanne wanted to feel satisfied with her performance at work and not constantly worry about not being good enough. She had a desire to become the head of the department but felt the goal was out of reach, and the job would surely go to someone else, someone who was "better" than her.

The seed of Susanne's lack of confidence in her ability was sown when she was two years old. She sat on the floor and played with her blocks. Her father sat down next to her and began to build a high tower with the blocks. Of course, she wanted to do the same but didn't succeed. The tower crashed again and again. Her dad laughed at her attempt, probably in an attempt to neutralize the whole situation. Susanne got angry and started screaming with frustration and disappointment. Eventually, her father lifted her away from the blocks and tried to get her interested in something else.

The interesting thing here is Susanne's interpretation. All children interpret differently, so I cannot generalize and say this is how all children would react. But in my work, I can notice patterns that show how many people react. In Susanne's case, the interpretation was, "I can't do what dad does." This was the first seed sown into her subconscious. Had Susanne been older and her conscious mind more developed, she would have been able to analyze and reason with herself. Had she under-stood that motor skills are not fully developed in a two-year-old and that she didn't have as much practical training on stacking things as her dad did, she would have realized she was not bad at building towers; she just hadn't practiced enough. With a little more training and experience, she could have built a tower as high as her dad did.

More events in Susanne's childhood where she compared herself to others were stacked on top of one another. In the end, they became her truth: She wasn't as good as everyone else. She began to live by this rule. Instead of focusing on learning and developing, she worried. Given that the brain wants to save energy, worrying isn't good. Being constantly worried takes lots of energy; and therefore, we can become very tired from it. Her inner mantra became "What I do isn't good enough. I can't do what others can," which eventually became the standard program in her brain. She got tired and couldn't keep up her focus on the job or immerse herself in things after work to develop. She began to feel depressed.

What Susanne didn't realize was that those she compared herself to were often older, had more experience, or had worked harder than she had. She didn't realize that her anxiety was consuming her energy, which could have instead been used to grow and learn more. When Susanne realized she could acquire knowledge and that she wasn't stupid or incompetent, the dissatisfaction disappeared. Her standard program changed, the worrying disappeared, the energy returned, and she could get better at her job. It only took her six months to become the head of the department.

When our standard program has become our identity, that's when we say, "This is how I am." Changing our thoughts, feelings, or behaviors is like letting go of part of our identity and can be a scary thing for many. We have invested a lot in creating our identity, and we would love to keep it, to know who we are. Changing our programming means letting go of our old identity and leaving behind the reality and security we created. It can feel empty to let go of our old thoughts, feelings, and behaviors. Who we have been has become a habit. We can become just as dependent on our own identity as we can become dependent on alcohol, cigarettes, shopping, or food.

You have a standard program your brain likes to use. If you try to change your thoughts, feelings, or behaviors with your conscious will, your subconscious programming will take you back to your default state after a while. You need to do a RESET in order to achieve a long-term change.

WHY DO WE KEEP A BAD STRATEGY?

There are many reasons why a bad strategy isn't replaced by a new and better one. Some of the most common reasons are:

- Sticking to habits and old rules saves energy. Running new tracks in the brain costs energy. Your conscious mind is usually activated only for new and important things.
- We have a negative default mode network (DMN) in the brain, our so-called autopilot, which makes us blind to new solutions or possibilities.
- We don't think we are worth feeling good.
- We suffer from learned helplessness and, therefore, believe we can't make a change.
- We are afraid of the unknown, the new, and the things we haven't learned.
- The brain likes what is familiar. It likes to know how things are, how things will be, and how it should respond. An old strategy can feel safe.
- As children, we create strategies for not having to experience negative emotions again. These patterns or programming are usually quite resistant to our attempts to change them, as they are linked to our survival. When a solution—a strategy—has been created that worked when the problem first arose, the subconscious may then believe that strategy is the best, or only, solution available—that the strategy is necessary for survival. The subconscious mind thinks, "Why should I change the strategy; it's working?"

Let's Look at an Example

You are six years old, and your parents have sent you to your room because you have been disobedient. You are angry, sad, and feeling guilty. All these horrible feelings are rushing around inside you. As you sit there pondering your fate, you see some candy lying on the table. To comfort yourself and to subdue some of your emotions, you eat the candy. For a little while, you feel better because you have distracted yourself from the emotions by eating.

In this situation, your brain can conclude that candy is the solution to feeling sad, and the subconscious creates a strategy where every time you feel a tough emotion, candy is chosen as the best solution. Since it worked the first time, it will certainly work well in the future. The subconscious can go so far as to see it as the only solution that works. When you're upset and try to calm yourself by taking a walk, taking a few deep breaths, talking to someone, or taking a bath, it won't work. The subconscious has decided that candy is the only solution. That's when you put on your jacket and shoes at 9:00 p.m. on a Sunday night and believe you just have to go down to the convenience store to shop for sweets, otherwise you'll go crazy. You know (logically) you won't go crazy, but your subconscious mind is telling you that you will if you don't get your candy. You know that candy doesn't really help, but your subconscious thinks it does. And, of course, it may feel like we are driven mad by our feelings sometimes. Actually, it's not the candy we want but a distraction from the tough feelings.

The child uses the resources available to solve his or her problem. A six-year-old cannot argue with his parents about what is a just punishment. A six-year-old cannot open a bottle of wine. A six-year-old can't call a friend and talk about his feelings. So the resource to take care of oneself and one's emotions, to distract oneself from the pain, can be the candy. It may be the only solution right then.

WHAT PROGRAMS ARE CONTROLLING YOU?

What your life looks like depends a lot on what programs your subconscious is running and what your matrix looks like. Your programming can either support or hinder you in life. Although the autopilot is good and simplifies your life, it's not very good if all your thoughts, feelings, and behaviors run automatically. Especially not if they are negative. In that case, you let the subconscious run the whole show, and you have lost control.

I had very poor programming. Coming from a religious upbringing, I had a narcissistic father and an emotionally closed-off mother. I was a sensitive child. Not a very successful combination. My dad was moody, so I often had to tiptoe around him. I remember when I was "disobedient." My mom would say, "Just wait until dad gets home." All day, I worried about my father's return and the punishment I would receive because I never knew how severe it would be. The punishment was rarely proportionate to the crime. Instead, it depended on what mood Dad was in when he came home from work. If he was happy, it was just a reprieve. If he was tired and in a bad mood, he pulled my pants down and spanked me for as long as he saw fit. This created the following programming in me:

- I have to be perfect because if I never do anything wrong, I won't be punished. This laid the foundation for senseless perfectionism for many years, which I have fortunately toned down a lot today.
- I can't influence the outcome. It's someone else (in my case, my dad) who decides the outcome. I'm powerless. This developed a great need for control in me. For many years, I suffered from general anxiety disorder (GAD) over things that *could* happen and things I couldn't affect. Today, I have practically eliminated all of my worry.

COMMON CONCLUSIONS AND STRATEGIES

When we, as children, continuously have bad and unpleasant experiences, we try to figure out why. We try to find an explanation for why the situations arise to avoid them. Because if we find an explanation, we might also find a solution. We need to understand what is happening to regain control. Since our conscious mind is not fully developed, our conclusions may not always be correct, nor the strategies very constructive.

Some examples of common conclusions:

- I am not loved, so I must be unlovable.
- They hurt me/punish me, so I have to be a bad person.
- Nobody cares about me; there must be something wrong with me.
- No one understands me. I'm alone.
- Nobody wants to be with me. I'm a burden.

- I'm not good enough. I'm unsuccessful. I'm worthless.
- I have to do this in order to get that.
- If I cry and make lots of noise, my needs will be met.
- If I become invisible, I will not be harmed.
- If I shut down, I don't have to feel the fear.
- If I'm kind, they will like me and take care of me.

Conclusions can become our themes in life. They create behavioral strategies that do not always benefit us. Some common strategies we use to deal with life are:

- We try to find compromises and ways to cooperate. We are good at mediating and making our moms and dads proud and happy.
- We retreat and disappear into our own world.
- We rebel or dominate. We get angry and create turmoil. Sometimes, we bully others.
- We are manipulating. We become smart and see what we need to do to get what we want.
- We overcompensate. We become accomplished and talented at what we do. We have a strong drive to succeed or try to satisfy others, becoming a so-called "people pleaser."

We use the strategy that works at the moment and we can also test the different strategies to see how the outside world reacts. A person who feels inferior or worthless can be outwardly dominant. A person with shame can be overly nice and giving, except to himself. A person with a lot of fear can become controlling, in an attempt to feel safe. When none of the above strategies work, we can create a combination of them.

YODA MOMENT

When I was thirteen, the first *Star Wars* movie premiered. I was completely in love. One of my favorite characters was Yoda. Although I didn't always understand his wisdom, something was awakened in me. As an adult, I have understood how wise Yoda was. During your Yoda Moments, I want you to reflect and listen to your inner wisdom about how things are in your life.

Here Comes Your First Yoda Moment.

As you understand, you can make a conscious choice and then discover that something within you has "taken over," and you are not acting as you intended to do. You have created strategies for managing things that have happened to avoid negative experiences in the future. These strategies create your personality (from the Greek *persona*, which means mask). Your strategies form your matrix, which influences your thoughts, feelings, decisions, and behaviors for the rest of your life—until you consciously change them.

Instead of wondering what is wrong with you or constantly criticizing yourself, ask yourself what has happened to you in your life that has created a negative impression and changed you. What has happened that has made you look at yourself as you do today, react in a certain way, slow down, or sabotage yourself in certain areas? What behaviors and strategies have you created to protect yourself from certain emotions?

Make an inventory of your beliefs. Pick up your journal and write, "Something I think about . . . (for example, myself) is . . ." Write freely. Don't think too much; don't judge. Don't censor. Write down everything you can think of, even if something sounds absurd or strange to you. Let your subconscious guide you.

Here are some suggestions on areas. Something I think about _____ is _____.

• Myself	• My opportunities	• The world
• My body	• My limitations	• Good and bad
• My health	• My attitudes	• Life
• My work	• My circumstances	• Universe / God
• My relationships	• Money	• The past
• My abilities	• Love	• The Future

Choose your **three** most important beliefs and ask yourself:

- How have these beliefs affected me in life?
- Who influenced me to have these beliefs?
- Did I consciously choose to believe this? When and why did I do it?
- What has been the benefit of having these beliefs? What did I gain from having them?
- What did I avoid by having these beliefs?
- Who would I be without these beliefs?
- What beliefs could I replace with more positive, beneficial, and strengthening alternatives?

Now make an inventory of strategies that you use in your everyday life, even though you know they don't work as well. Feel free to pick up your journal and write down your reflections:

- What behaviors and strategies are you using today that are not working satisfactorily?
- What in your childhood has led you to create the strategies you still use as an adult?
- What situations and which people trigger your non-functioning strategies?
- What behaviors and strategies have you created to protect yourself from certain emotions?
- What behaviors and strategies would you like to have?

You can actually train your brain so you don't always react automatically according to old programming. In the next chapter, you will find #mindhacks that will help you replace your old beliefs and strategies with new and more productive ones. It's time for you to hack the code, your matrix, and do a RESET on your standard programs. It's not an instant fix. To re-code your old thoughts, feelings, and behaviors takes time, but it is definitely worth it.

CHAPTER 2 IN 60 SECONDS

- The subconscious mind is like a large database where everything you have learned, experienced, and interpreted is stored.
- The matrix is the program that controls your thoughts, feelings, and behaviors. Your beliefs are the rules of the game.
- Your subconscious will always run the program that it thinks is best for your survival, even if you consciously think otherwise.
- Your programming has no expiration date. The strategies become your habits.
- To save energy, the brain automates. Your autopilot controls 95 percent of your day.
- The brain likes what is familiar, that which creates a sense of security and control. That's why you keep old strategies and stay in your comfort zone, even if you're not happy.

READY TO RE:DO?

I will now teach you some effective Jedi Mind Tricks to *reset* your matrix. During this process, you will find hacks that become your favorites and hacks that do not appeal to you as much. This is perfectly okay; you don't need to use all of them. Pick out the #mindhacks you like the most and practice consistently.

You need to practice and have a dose of patience. Pay attention, as the changes tend to sneak up on you. It is quite normal if you sometimes take a few steps forward and then take a step back. This is what the flow of change looks like. Have a journal close at hand, where you write down your reflections and the changes you notice.

Be not afraid of growing slowly; be afraid only of standing still.
Chinese Proverb

CHAPTER 3

HACKING THE CODE

Your brain believes what you tell it.
Carefully choose what you think and say to yourself.

According to The National Science Foundation in the United States, we have about 60–70,000 thoughts per day. That's 2,500 thoughts per hour, of which 2,250 thoughts per hour are the same as we thought the day before. 2,000 of those thoughts per hour are negative. We are not even aware of 95 percent of our thoughts.

Whether these numbers are correct or not, there are many thoughts running around in our heads. I remember my first thought after hearing this: "How can I replace all of these?" I promise, it is possible! It's not like I always walk around thinking, "It's possible. I can do it. I'm good enough. I'm a good person," but my standard mood is more positive today. I am happier, more content, more confident, and calmer. You will soon learn how I managed to change this.

NEGATIVE THOUGHTS TAKE PRECEDENCE

Some of the most common reasons we often have so many negative thoughts are:

- Thinking negatively and worrying is a survival strategy, a remnant from our ancestors from thousands of years ago. Their everyday lives were quite dangerous, filled with many threats, and it was important to notice them to survive. It was also crucial to plan for the future to increase your chance of survival, hence the worry. That is why our brain today has a negative preset. We simply notice dangers and problems more easily than positive events. Our ancient brain does not understand the difference between having to run away from a lion, hunting food for the winter, protecting us from a storm, worrying about what might happen at work next week, not being on time for the bus, or stressing about bills that need to be paid. Our ability to plan for the future is a double-edged sword. It gives us the ability to avoid things we don't want to happen, but it can also make us worry about the future before something has happened.
- We have been programmed by our parents, teachers, authorities, and society. If our surroundings have a pattern of negative thinking, we will learn that pattern.
- It becomes a habit to think negatively. For example, if you think you're not good enough, your thoughts will sound something like this: "I can't do it. Nobody likes me. It's not possible. I always fail. I'm not good enough." Eventually, you will have a negative default setting that runs on autopilot, and it will be activated when you encounter different people and situations.
- Many people are unknowingly addicted to negative thinking. Can you really become addicted to negative thoughts? Yes! When not-so-good things happen to us, we can feel helpless. One way to avoid feeling helpless is to turn our negative thinking into our standard setting. When we are negative, it protects us from being disappointed when problems arise and disasters occur. We have already told ourselves that it won't turn out well or that it won't work. We already know the outcome, and this way we can fulfill our need of having control.

THE LENS THROUGH WHICH YOU SEE THE WORLD

We all protect ourselves from disappointment to some degree. Let's take an example. You are bullied in school as a child. After a while, you will be on your guard against all children because they can hurt you. You start to have negative thoughts about yourself and others. There is something wrong with you. You are a failure, others are stupid, or you cannot trust people. You lose your faith in other people. You are convinced that you cannot contribute to the world in any way. You become more withdrawn and avoid social situations. You are looking for the worst rather than seeing the best in others. Your negative default setting is installed, and you see the world through a dirty lens. Cleaning your lens by creating a positive mindset is, therefore, super important.

CLIENT STORY

I Can't Do It

Elsa was a smart and happy ten-year-old. When Elsa came to me, she had developed a bad habit of worrying. She worried that things would go wrong, that she would embarrass herself, and that she wouldn't be able to handle challenging situations.

During the session, we discovered that her concerns had begun at a scout camp. Elsa woke up in the middle of the night and couldn't fall back asleep. She was afraid to get up alone and didn't know what she was supposed or allowed to do. So, she remained in bed, awake and perfectly still, until morning. It felt like an eternity.

When Elsa told the leaders the next day that she wanted to call her parents and go home, she wasn't allowed to do so. She had to continue to worry for a few more days. Elsa concluded that it was not worthwhile to tell anyone about her worries—no one listened to her or helped her. This conclusion was saved in her subconscious, and a new strategy must now be created to relieve the anxiety and feeling of helplessness.

By chance, Elsa discovered a few months later that if she said, "I can't do it," she didn't have to do it. She didn't have to do things she didn't want to do. This new strategy was formed. After a while, this setting was run in all sorts of situations because it worked. As soon as Elsa encountered something new, where there was a risk that no one would listen to her needs, that she wouldn't get the chance to decide for herself, or where she didn't really know what to do, her subconscious checked the directory for a strategy to use.

It said: That's right. This is where I'm going to use "I can't do it" because then everyone backs away. But when Elsa constantly said, "I can't do it," it became a truth in her mind, and she began to lose confidence. Elsa understood that saying "I can't do it" was not a good thing because it meant debasing herself. Her shoulders fell down, and she admitted she was disappointed in herself when she didn't do things that she knew she could do.

Elsa and I decided we should delete this setting and that it was better if she said "I don't want to," "I need help," "I'm scared," or "I need time" instead. Elsa's new setting was to replace "I can't do it" with "I know I can do it," dare to ask for extra time and help, and say no. I explained to Elsa's parents that sometimes she needed a little more time, take smaller steps, and not be compared to others when it came to what she could or couldn't do. They would need to listen to her and allow her to express her will, even though she could not always get her will through. With the parents' backing, it worked out well.

This is a good example of how a negative thought can arise, which is then transformed into a strategy that eventually starts to create problems. The subconscious finds a solution that seems good at the moment, but the strategy becomes a barrier after a while.

★ YODA MOMENT

Now, it's time to be honest with yourself. Take a look at your inventory of beliefs and strategies, which you created in Chapter 2.

- What negative thoughts are circulating in your head?
- What do you tell yourself about yourself?
- Have you become addicted to your negative thoughts to protect yourself?
- What has happened in your life that has caused your negative thoughts, beliefs, and strategies to appear?
- What have your negative thoughts, beliefs, and strategies cost you earlier in your life? What do they cost you today? What do you think they will cost you in the future?

Reflect and write down your thoughts in your journal.

By being honest about how you sometimes think negatively, you own your negativity. You acknowledge it, and do not blame other people or circumstances. You take responsibility. When we blame something outside ourselves, we lose our POWER and our ability to change our programs. We are completely in the hands of others and what is happening in our environment. But once you understand that you can choose what you think and how you react, you take back your POWER. Be kind to yourself. You have taught yourself to have these catastrophic thoughts, negative thoughts, and worries. It is possible to unlearn them. Of course, there will be moments when you react and cannot think the "right way," but with practice and patience, you will become better at choosing a different thought, a different reaction, and a different behavior.

⚙ JEDI MIND TRICKS

Now, we are going to practice shifting from your negative standard mode to your executive mode, where you have an opportunity to choose how you view things, situations, and people. You will learn some effective #mindhacks that will make you an active thinker and help build a positive standard mode. If you practice regularly, it won't take long for you to notice changes in your way of thinking, and this new way will soon become natural.

O⟲ HACK #1

CRUSH THE ANTs

To break your negative standard setting, you need to be aware of what you are thinking. Your brain believes in what you tell it; therefore, you have to choose the words you tell yourself with care. What you say about yourself, others, and the situations you encounter will be the lens you look through. What you say about yourself is confirmed by how you act, what people and situations you attract, and how you deal with them.

The first step is, therefore, to put the headlamp on and notice when you think negatively about yourself, your surroundings, or the situations you are in. You should hunt "the ANTs" (automatic negative thoughts). What does the dialogue sound like in your head? Which negative thoughts usually arise? What in your environment triggers you to think, feel, or act in a not-so-good way? Triggers have a tendency to activate your negative default setting. A trigger can be anything: what someone says or does, a scent, a season, and even a door . . .

CLIENT STORY

The Door is Dangerous

Cecilia loved to ride her horse. However, there was one part of it that she didn't like - to ride past the riding hall door. Every time the door was in sight, Cecilia felt her horse start to tense and she became afraid of being thrown off the horse. Her goal was to keep calm so that she could help her horse in the best way.

The first thing we discovered was that Cecilia tensed up before the horse did, not the other way around. So why did she get tense every time they would pass the door? Was it because she knew that the horse was going to cause a problem and there was a risk that she would fall? No, the reason was a completely different one. Cecilia's childhood was riddled with fighting, alcohol, and grabby men. Every day when she came home from school and put her hand on the door handle, she tensed up with fear. She never knew what she would have to face. Her subconscious saved the information that doors were negative and dangerous. They could lead to problems. The door became the trigger that remained thirty years later. As she approached a door, her subconscious warned her about a "potential danger."

Cecilia was surprised about the root of her problems with the door but could recognize that she often became nervous when she walked through doors leading to buildings, premises, and others' homes.

To speed up the healing, she adopted a mantra she repeated every time she approached a door. "I'm safe today. I see doors as opportunities." Today, Cecilia meets all doors with a sense of calm.

 Feel free to think about what triggers you to react a certain way. When you know your triggers, you can often trace them back in time to when you were a child.

Create Good Anchor Thoughts

It's time to "crush the ANTs." Negative thought patterns are just a habit. You don't wake up in the morning and think, "Today, I will only think bad thoughts about myself." Negativity arises when you let the thoughts drift away and pay no attention to them. As soon as you realize you're having negative thoughts, say *stop*. This will activate your prefrontal cortex, which is your executive boss, the one who can break the habit. Simply tell your thoughts, "That's enough," and replace them with more constructive ones. The new constructive thoughts become your anchor thoughts, which you will use as soon as you feel negative or worried. Anchor thoughts are a powerful way to take control of your thoughts as they begin to swirl in a downward spiral. You can't always control what is happening around you or how you feel, but you can definitely learn to control your thoughts.

- The anchor thought is a thought that makes you feel happy, calm, confident, and strong.

- The anchor thought is planned, and it gives you a winning edge when you need it. Create a set of anchor thoughts you can use in different situations. It's not always easy to come up with something positive or constructive in the moment.

- The anchor thought should be realistic for you to accept it. You've probably heard of positive affirmations. "I'm happy. I'm enough. I'm successful. I'm fantastic . . ." Studies show affirmations don't always work. They can even make you feel worse. Why? Because our belief system is very defensive. If a statement can be contained within our belief system, we accept it. When a claim falls outside our belief system, we reject it. If you say you are fantastic but have programming that says the opposite, it will say, "Bullsh—! We don't believe in that." You will reject all claims that say the opposite of your programming. There is another reason why positive thinking doesn't always work. With what part do you think positive thoughts? The conscious part, which only controls 5 percent of your day. As you probably understand, the conscious mind doesn't stand a great chance against the subconscious, which has a 400-billion-bit processor and controls 95 percent of your day. But there are ways to access the subconscious, and you will learn more about that in Chapter 8. There are affirmations that work—namely the ones you have created yourself and that are positive and true for you. Since you can choose your own anchor thoughts, choose the ones that strengthen you and create a wonderful feeling in your body. Since an anchor thought creates a specific feeling or experience, you can also ask yourself what emotion or experience you would like to have within a certain area. If you imagine that feeling right now, what anchor thought creates that feeling?

Since the anchor thoughts should be planned, you need to think of which ones work for you in advance. Make a list of your qualities that you find valuable, in any field.

Examples

- Relationships: I am loyal. I am caring. I am loving. I am good at taking care of my home . . .
- Work: I am responsible. I learn quickly. I enjoy self-development. I am solution-driven . . .
- General qualities: I look for solutions. I'm helpful. I'm listening. I'm open to new things . . .

The best way to do this is to write a short sentence for each quality you think you have. Writing makes it easier for the brain to absorb the positive information. Why is this quality important? Why do you value it? Why do others value it? How have you used this quality in your life? How would you like to express it in the future? With a positive anchor thought, you are reminded of your self-worth. You are good. You are capable. You have a lot to offer.

Below you will find a number of general suggestions for how to transform a negative thought into a more constructive one. You can also select a negative belief that you discovered using the questions in Chapter 2, and replace it with a constructive anchor thought. Only use anchor thoughts that sound right to you. The best way is to create your own. Think of Cecilia who created a positive anchor thought as she passed through doors: "I'm safe today. I see doors as opportunities."

Negative Thought	Constructive Thought
I have nothing to offer.	I can offer . . . (a quality of yours).
I'm not smart enough.	If I learn, then I can do anything.
I'm not good enough.	I do my best. I always try. I am . . . (a quality of yours).
What if I disappoint them?	I do what makes me proud of myself.
I'm too young.	I have plenty of time to learn.
I'm too old.	I have plenty of experience. I choose to be curious.
I can't do it.	I can't do it at this moment, but I'm learning.
I'm afraid. I don't dare.	I take small steps. I'm building up my courage.
It's hopeless.	I will find a way that works. I will let go of what doesn't work.

I have failed.	What have I learned?
I couldn't do it.	I have managed to . . . (something you are proud of).

Creating anchor thoughts is a way to upgrade your language. When you create a positive standard setting, you will build a buffer of positivity that makes you more emotionally resilient. So, go ahead and smash all the ANTs!

O—⚲ HACK #2

VISUALIZE LIKE A NAVY SEAL

The interesting thing about our brain is that it has a "flaw," which we can use to our advantage. The flaw is that our brain doesn't know the difference between reality and fiction. In other words, our brain cannot differentiate between something we think about and something that actually happens. Try it! Think of something you are afraid of. Imagine what scares you, and make it really big and real. If you do it right, you will begin to experience anxiety or nervousness in your body.

The fact that our brains cannot distinguish between reality and fiction becomes clear if we think of certain things we fear. If we don't like flying or making speeches, our brain and body can respond to thoughts of the flight or the speech several months before it's time. We can get worried and nervous, or even scared and anxious, just from the thought of what we're going to do. The positive side is that the opposite is also true.

Instead, think of something positive you are looking forward to. Or think of something that has happened in your life that made you truly happy or proud of yourself. You will notice that you are experiencing feelings of wellbeing, joy, and pride.

An effective way of making your brain more positive and open to new possibilities is to visualize. A client of mine taught her nine-year-old son the art of visualizing because he was constantly worried that he wouldn't be able to do the exercises at the gymnastics lesson. To reverse the negative spiral, he visualized what exciting tricks he was able to learn, how he got help from the teacher, how strong he became, and how much he had to tell his mother when she came to pick him up. After a few weeks, the anxiety was completely gone. That is the power of visualization.

When you visualize, you control your thoughts. You are training to go from your default mode, your autopilot, to an active mode. Just like when Morpheus and Neo train in the dojo in the movie *The Matrix*. There are several studies that show how effective visualization is.

In one study, basketball players were divided into three groups, and their ability to make free throws was tested. Group 1 trained for twenty minutes a day. Group 2 visualized making free throws but didn't actually practice them. Group 3 neither trained nor visualized. Interestingly, the group of basketball players who visualized their free throws was almost as good as the group of basketball players who trained making free throws for twenty minutes daily.

Our brain has a filter system, which makes us collect information, and confirms or proves what we already believe; all other information is blocked. The filter system is called the reticular activation system (RAS). Its job is to go through the day and point out any evidence that confirms our beliefs. So, if we walk around and believe we are not good enough or no one likes us, this filter system will look for evidence that we are not good enough and no one likes us. We simply prove to ourselves that we are right. The system also only allows information that is relevant to us at the moment. Without this system, our brains would let in all the information without screening it, and we would probably explode. Visualization changes the filter system and allows us to open up to new possibilities. We become more positive, so we can filter the world in a more constructive way. For example, we can begin to see solutions to problems, which previously seemed impossible to solve, or see a person's good qualities, not just the bad ones that annoy us.

You can use the visualization directly in the morning when you wake up to set a positive tone for the day. You can visualize before a meeting, a task, or a challenge. Personally, I like to start my day with a powerful visualization of how I want the day to develop or how I want to feel. To take advantage of the visualization, you only need to close your eyes for thirty to sixty seconds and immerse yourself in the experience. I call it snuggling. Make it colorful and as vivid as you can. Loading your visualization with positive emotions is important. If you think positively, such as "my meeting with the customer will go well," "I'm feeling good," or "I'm a good person," but still *feel* fear, dissatisfaction, or inadequacy, the thought will never pass the brainstem and into the body because the thought is not in line with the emotional state of the body. When you think positively during your visualization, you program the circuits in your brain to think in a way that is good for you. If you also load the experience with positive emotions, you will teach your body how your future feels, and your body will be more likely to move into the future. How you think and feel creates your inner state.

The trick is to have confidence in the fact that things will turn out the way you want them to. Don't hope that the desired result will happen but really believe it is already true. I practice gratitude, as if the positive result has already happened. If you are grateful for what comes to you in the future, then the body believes that it is getting something now, and it is more likely to move forward. Another important component is that you visualize the steps you take toward the goal, not just the finish line itself.

You can also add a trigger. For example, when you feel the warm stream from the shower, you visualize the wonderful feeling of having a strong body and see yourself taking action to get there. Here are some examples of themes you can visualize:

Examples

- How your day will be.
- You reaching for a specific goal.
- What steps you take to reach your goal.
- Everything positive that you have in your life.
- The person you want to be in a year.
- What you do every day to be healthy.
- How your relationship with your partner is flourishing.
- How you are positive and seize opportunities.
- How you solve and manage a challenge.

You can visualize anywhere; the important thing is that you are undisturbed. Make visualization wonderful. Even Navy SEALs, the US Navy's toughest guys and one of the world's toughest elite troop, often brought in for impossibly difficult assignments, learn to visualize how they will succeed in their challenges and the steps they take toward their goals.

O⊸ HACK #3

A WINNING MORNING

Whatever you choose to do in the first few minutes of the morning sets the tone for the whole day. The beginning of the day affects your mood, productivity, focus, and how you look at yourself and your life. Shawn Achor, one of the world's leading experts on happiness, states that if you consume three minutes of negative news or stressful emails and text messages in the morning, you run a 50 percent greater risk that by the end of the day, you will find that your day has been bad. Negative information in the morning causes your brain to look for negative things during the day. In addition, you can increase your productivity during the day by about 30 percent if you don't check the mail in the first hour of the morning. Most successful people have morning routines that allow them to perform at peak levels for the rest of the day. Visualizing, like you just learned, is a winning morning routine.

No Cell Phone in the Bedroom

Your morning starts the night before. When you go to bed, it is not wise to have your cell phone in the bedroom. According to Anders Hansen, a chief physician in psychiatry, having the cellphone near the bed is enough to disrupt our mental bandwidth. The bedroom is for sleeping and cozy time, so no cell phone! Charge it in another room and raise the volume so you wake up with the alarm in the morning. Or buy a regular alarm clock. Many of us are so addicted to our cellphones that we surf in the middle of the night, and it's the first thing we grab in the morning. If the first thing your brain encounters each day is a blue screen, it will be overwhelmed with impressions and start rushing. If you don't have control over your morning, you do not have control over your mindset, your day or, by extension, your life.

No Snoozing

When the alarm clock goes off, get out of bed straight away. Snoozing is not good for the brain; it can ruin your sleep cycle. A sleep cycle is about ninety to 110 minutes long, and after a certain number of cycles, you wake up, ready to face the day. If you snooze, a new sleep cycle starts. When it's interrupted ten minutes later, the brain gets stuck in the current cycle, and it can take up to four hours to shake off the sleep inertia. When you are in this sleepy fog, the brain does not work properly. Your cognitive functions are slow, and you don't make the best decisions.

So, the cellphone is out of the way, and you are out of bed. What happens next?

Morning Rituals

Don't allow the world to steal your first precious minutes in the morning. Prepare yourself so you have more access to your executive mode, where you think and act consciously. Focus on something positive that is important to you, to fuel you up with your own POWER. This is where morning rituals come in. With these, you prioritize yourself for a while. This is important because when you open your computer, pick up your cellphone, or meet others, you let the world in, allowing it to pull you in all possible directions.

The morning rituals you are about to learn will help you to grow, reach your goals, create focus, be productive, find balance, unleash your creativity, and have clarity. You are preparing to activate your executive mode.

Morning rituals may include:

- Visualization
- Meditation
- Collecting gold nuggets (scanning for positive things)
- Writing in a journal (reflections, gratitude, goals or challenges)
- Planning your day (choose something that is important to you and set your priority for the day)
- Exercise or walking
- Reading or listening to something that expands you
- Engaging in something that boosts your mood and energy

Start small and with what feels easiest or most fun. Don't worry about the goal. For example, if you decide to meditate, ignore the recommendations that you should meditate for at least twenty minutes to get the full effect. Start with one minute, or five. Instead of goals, follow your curiosity and energy. Experiment and be open to variety.

How Much Time Do You Need?

You decide for yourself how much time you have. Somewhere between ten and thirty minutes is usually enough. The important thing is that you are realistic. If you have family and children, you may not be able to devote a lot of time each morning to yourself. All of my morning rituals take about one hour. But I have (or rather take) that time. It has taken me a while to get my rituals in place, and sometimes, I need to adjust them based on my life situation. When I'm traveling, I'm happy if I can do half of my morning rituals. Even if you lose your good habits from time to time, just pick them up again.

Depending on how much time you can spare in the morning, you can use the model 5/5/5, 10/10/10, or 20/20/20. Experiment. You can, of course, exchange the different segments with others that suit you better. The important thing is that you create a morning ritual that strengthens you for the day.

5/5/5	10/10/10	20/20/20
Reflection 5 min	Reflection 10 min	Reflection 20 min
Activity 5 min	Activity 10 min	Activity 20 min
Knowledge 5 min	Knowledge 10 min	Knowledge 20 min
TOTAL 15 min	**TOTAL 30 min**	**TOTAL 60 min**

Reflection

Choose one of the following: meditation, journaling, collecting gold nuggets, practicing gratitude, visualization, or planning your day. Meditation creates focus, calm, clarity, and energy. Through visualization, you control your thoughts, becoming more positive and in line with your goals. Collecting gold nuggets increases your joy, and you get a dopamine shower. Writing in a journal helps you clarify your thoughts and feelings and see how you might develop.

One of my favorite activities during reflection time is to plan my day. Take five minutes and decide on one thing to do during the day that will move you forward in your development and toward your goals. Choose something important to you and set your priority for the day. If there is a risk that you will not be able to carry out your activity during the day, I recommend you do it immediately in the morning. Your mental focus, energy level, and willpower are at peak levels in the morning. You don't want to spend your best hours of the day doing your least important activities.

Activity

Exercise, sweat, breathe. Moving directly in the morning helps your brain clear away cortisol. BDNF is released, a fertilizer for the brain, which increases your focus and speeds up your learning and growing. Movement gives you a dopamine shower, releases serotonin, and increases your metabolism. Just five minutes of yoga, a short walk, or a run are enough.

Knowledge

Articles, books, and movies. Learn something every morning. Knowledge gives you insight, and you grow as a person. You increase your opportunities to develop and increase your inspiration and creativity. You can contribute knowledge to others and help them grow.

Create Energy

If you wake up and feel that your mood is not the best or that your energy is low, then prioritize doing something that gives you energy and gets you in a good mood. It does not matter if it is calm or energy-rich activities; choose something that boosts both mood and energy.

My favorite way to get my energy flowing is to take a contrast shower. I take turns running cold and hot water for five minutes. Ten rounds where I alternate twenty seconds cold with ten seconds warm. I become alert and feel the energy flowing through my body, while creating a good mood. Contrast showers also have a number of other benefits. They strengthen the immune system, reduce inflammation in the body, build up stress resistance, lower blood sugar, burn fat, improve adrenal and thyroid function, and improve sleep quality. If you want to know more about how cold temperatures and breathing can affect your brain, I recommend you read more about Wim Hof "The Iceman." He's an exciting character with whom I have had the privilege of hiking and doing ice baths.

Make the Decision

If you hear yourself saying, "I don't have the energy" or "I don't feel like doing it" or "I don't have the time," the morning rituals are too long or complicated. Break them down to something you can do. If you wait for the right time to be motivated, then you have lost the battle. You may not always feel like getting out of the warm bed. Motivation comes as a result of having done something so many times that it becomes a need because you see the results of your efforts. Make the decision to do your morning rituals. It will change your life.

O⊸ HACK #4

BOOST YOUR WILLPOWER

Your willpower is not at the same level throughout the day. With every decision you make, every task you perform, your willpower is weakened. Did you know that when you go to bed at night you have made an average of 35,000 decisions that day? That's why we usually can't resist that glass of wine, the snacks, or a splurge of chocolate in the evening. That's why we don't want to put on our jogging shoes and go for a run after work. Our brain simply can't make good decisions.

Social psychologist Roy F. Baumeister, who developed the notion of decision fatigue, argues that our brain is affected by analysis paralysis. The longer the day goes on, the less willpower and self-control we can muster. Just as our muscles get tired after a long workout, so does our brain after a long day. When our brain is tired, it saves energy by making impulsive decisions . . . or no decisions at all. That's why we sometimes say to our partners, "I don't care what we eat for dinner, you decide."

Thus, there is a link between decision fatigue and poor willpower and self-control. When we are experiencing decision fatigue, we have a harder time controlling our impulses. Our self-control decreases, and we become emotionally unstable, underperform, lose our stamina, and may even fail to perform our tasks.

Especially in this digital age, where we are flooded with information, the brain has to make decisions all of the time. Should we pay attention to the incoming information or ignore it? So even when we ignore information, the brain makes a decision. As the day progresses and more decisions are made, the brain begins to take shortcuts to save energy. One shortcut is to act impulsively when making decisions. It doesn't always have to be that we make the wrong decision, but we make the decision that is safest or most convenient for us. So . . . I stay on the couch and run tomorrow instead. The brain will favor the short-term benefits. We will choose the alternative that is the quickest to finish or that feels best in the moment. The willpower to get things done the right way isn't strong enough to do what we know is best for us in the long run.

There are several ways to counteract fatigue. With a few simple routines and breaks during the day, you can replenish your willpower and increase your productivity.

Take a Break from the Noise

There is a reason why some of your best ideas and decisions come up when you are in the shower or out for a walk. When you pull away from the noise of the day for a moment, you free your prefrontal cortex, the thinking part of the brain and your chief executive. Your prefrontal cortex is responsible for logical thinking, and it uses willpower to overcome impulses, which is important during decision fatigue. By giving the brain a break, you improve the neural connections, and you will be able to make better decisions.

Introduce Procedures That Minimize the Number of Decisions

Former US President Barack Obama understood the importance of minimizing the number of decisions per day to avoid decision fatigue:

"You see that I only wear gray or blue suits. I try to reduce the number of decisions. I don't want to make decisions about what to eat or what clothes to put on. I have too many other decisions to make. You need to focus your decision-making energy. You need to create routines. You can't go through the day distracted by trivialities."

Get inspired by Obama, and create effective habits and routines that help you save brain energy. Prepare as much as you can the night before, so you don't have to make too many decisions the next day. Prepare tomorrow's clothes, put your exercise bag out, pack healthy snacks in the bag—in case cravings strike—or create a winning morning as you learned in Chapter 3. Your willpower and self-control are usually strongest in the morning because then the fatigue of decision has not turned up. Therefore, it is best to do the most important things first. If you have also made plans the night before for the day, you have a winning concept.

Schedule Your Daily Tasks

Instead of deciding several times a day what to do, in what order and when, schedule your tasks and do them at the same time each day. For example, at 10:00 a.m., you always check your mail, at 1:00 p.m., you take your daily walk, and before bedtime, you prepare your morning smoothie so you can easily start the next morning in a healthy way.

O⊸ HACK #5

COLLECTING GOLD NUGGETS

Psychologist Sonja Lyubomirsky and her colleagues have concluded that as much as 40 percent of our happiness can be controlled. You are not just your genes and surroundings. Collecting gold nuggets is an effective way to steer your brain away from the autopilot and turn it to the direct mode, your executive mode, and start looking positively at life.

Collecting gold nuggets is about letting our neurons (brain cells) fire a little longer and more intensely around positive experiences, so they can be saved in our long-term memories. Collecting gold nuggets makes us more optimistic; we begin to see the positive in life as the dopamine and serotonin levels increase, and we feel more satisfied with life. Collecting gold nuggets is about teaching the brain to scan the world in a new way. Instead of searching for threats, we teach it to scan for positive things. In this way, we help the brain shift the focus from the negative to the positive. Research shows that you can experience these effects after just three weeks.

We need to help our brain a little extra to incorporate positive experiences because it's more difficult to transform positive experiences into long-lasting neural structures. Positive experiences use the standard memory systems and move the experience from short-term memory to long-term memory. This transfer requires that the experience be kept long enough in the short-term memory buffer system to be converted into a long-term memory. This is where the problem arises. We usually do not stay long enough in our positive experiences for them to be coded into neural structures in our long-term memories. We need to keep the experience in the short-term memory buffer system for twenty to thirty seconds for it to become a long-term memory. We simply need to marinate in the positive experience a little longer. When we stay in the positive experience for a long time, the part of the brain called the striatum is stimulated, which is directly linked to maintaining our positive moods. When we marinate in positive emotions, we strengthen the brain's ability to retain the positive emotions for longer periods.

How often have you stayed in the positive feeling for twenty to thirty seconds after getting a compliment? How often do you allow yourself to enjoy something that you have done well? Or is it just be a "yes . . . that was fine" and then you move on? Do you see your efforts or focus on what remains to be done? What do you usually think of at the end of the day? The twenty things that went well or the one thing that went poorly? What you did during the day or what you didn't do during the day? Do you feel grateful for what you have, or do you just see what is missing? If you are like most of us, you adhere to the latter. Our brain scans for threats and the negativity of old habits to keep us safe, and once the brain finds a threat, it isolates it and loses overall perspective. By contrast, if we gather positive experiences and feel gratitude for them, studies from University of California, Los Angeles's (UCLA's) Mindfulness Awareness Research Center show that we change the molecular structure of the brain, make the gray brain substance work better, and become healthier and happier.

Neuropsychologist Rick Hanson describes how to collect gold nuggets in three simple steps:

1. Look for good facts: something positive that happened during the day (also something positive that happened inside yourself), something you are grateful for, or something you have done that you are proud of. It can be small things—a good cup of coffee, a compliment, a hug from your child, beautiful weather, a phone call to a friend who needed you, or

even a negative thought that was exchanged for a positive one. General, positive things you are grateful for are less effective, such as gratitude for your family or a job or a healthy body. Detailed information creates greater impact on your brain. "I'm grateful for my daughter's hug because it makes me feel loved. I'm proud of the praise my boss gave me today because it makes me feel valued at work. I'm glad the sun was shining today because it gives me energy." When you experience something good, allow yourself to feel good. If you forget to enjoy the moment, you can pick up the memory of the experience a little later when you have time, for example when you have a reflection moment. I collect gold nuggets just before I fall asleep, when the brain is especially receptive to taking in new things. An added benefit is that I fall asleep with a positive tone. My favorite is to feel gratitude for everything I have in life.

2. Hold on and enjoy the experience for twenty to thirty seconds, without being distracted. Load the experience with emotions: see, hear, and feel. The longer you hold the experience and charge it with strong emotions, the more neurons are fired simultaneously, and the memory track becomes stronger. It's like depositing money into your bank account. You become filled with positivity.

3. Absorb the experience, and let it sink deep into you. I call it bathing or snuggling in the experience. Everyone does this in different ways. Some feel a warm feeling spread in the chest. Some visualize a golden light that fills the body from the top down, healing all the holes of pain. Some imagine a diamond placed in a treasure chest. Some envision being swept up in a warm blanket that fill them with positive thoughts.

Gratitude Changes the Brain

My absolute favorite variant of collecting gold nuggets is gratitude. Gratitude is a natural antidepressant miracle. When we feel gratitude, our brain releases dopamine and serotonin, two important signaling substances that control our emotions and make us feel good. The Mindfulness Awareness Research Center at UCLA has shown that if we practice gratitude regularly, we change the neural structures of the brain, and we feel happier and more satisfied. Feel-good hormones are released and affect most of our body. Our limbic system, which is responsible for our emotional experiences, is balanced. Our sleep improves because the hypothalamus, which regulates sleep, among other things, works better. Gratitude can cure stress, anxiety, and depression by reducing stress hormones in the body and regulating the autonomic nervous system. Gratitude strengthens our ability to deal with difficulties in life, and we build a mental and emotional strength. The list can be made even longer, but I will stop here.

When Should You Collect Your Gold Nuggets?

Collect gold nuggets every day—in the morning to start the day in a positive way, during the day when something positive happens, or you can do it, as I do, by picking out some positive experiences from the day when you go to bed at night.

Can You Do This with Others?

Feel free to invite your partner, family, and children. Maybe you can gather around the dinner table or before you all go to sleep to imprint positive thoughts together. See if you can notice the oddly positive things. Make it a game to call out new things every day, and be creative in saving your gold nuggets. A client of mine saved her best gold nuggets in a jar. When she experienced something special, something she wanted to remember, she wrote it down on a piece of paper and put it in the jar. On New Year's Eve, she emptied the jar of notes and read everything she had written. What a wonderful way to end the year!

What To Do If You Don't Find Any Gold Nuggets?

It doesn't matter if you don't find many gold nuggets; it is the scanning itself that counts. When you scan for positive experiences, the neurons in the brain become more efficient over time, so it becomes easier to find them because there are always gold nuggets in our lives.

If You Feel a Resistance Looking for Gold Nuggets

Think about why you feel a resistance. Is there an underlying blockage and where does it come from? Do you use "I don't feel any difference" as an excuse to give up? You may have a belief that you don't deserve happiness and joy or a fear that if you do well, you might lose it all. Keep looking for gold nuggets, even if you feel a resistance. Over time, it will fill you with positivity.

CHAPTER 3 IN 60 SECONDS

- Negative thoughts take precedence, as the ability to see dangers can ensure your survival.
- All disaster thoughts, negative thoughts, and worries are just habits. It's possible to correct them.
- Your brain believes what you tell it. Carefully choose what you think and say to yourself.
- **Crush the ANTs.** Say STOP and replace your automatic negative thoughts with positive, constructive, and realistic anchor thoughts, which you have prepared.
- **Visualize like a Navy Seal**. Visualize for thirty to sixty seconds each morning to steer your thoughts and feelings toward a positive active state.
- **A winning morning.** Establish morning rituals to help you create a successful day. No cellphone in the bedroom and no snooze button in the morning.
- **Boost your willpower.** Avoid decision fatigue and impulse actions by creating routines and taking breaks during the day.
- **Collect gold nuggets.** Collect what has been good during the day. Close your eyes, make the experience vivid, and "snuggle" for twenty to thirty seconds.

CHAPTER 4

LET GO OF THE BRAKE

*Good self-esteem and self-confidence are not something
you either have or don't. They are something you build over time
and constantly exercise, just like with your physical fitness.*

As babies, we usually felt valued. When we smiled, someone typically smiled back. Adults smiled at us for just being there and bringing joy and wonder. We were perfect even if we had poop in our diaper, porridge in our hair, and couldn't do any household chores.

We love the attention—often demand it—because we believe we are worth it. When my goddaughter, Aleta, was five years old, and I wasn't giving her enough attention while listening to her, she used to put her little hand on my cheek, turn my face toward her, look me in the eyes, and when she felt she had my full attention, she continued to talk.

When we mastered new things, we received praise. We stumbled over our first words and got praise, even though we couldn't say the words properly. We took our first steps and were greeted by smiles. We started eating by ourselves and received applause. Our parents were excited about how adorable we were. No one mentioned our failures, the fact that we said the words incorrectly, that we kept falling over, or that we missed our mouth with the fork half of the time. We were fully charged with confidence. But then one day, the praise began to decline. We were faced with more demands. Adults start saying *no*, and we were scolded if we didn't obey them. We started school, and demands were increasing from everyone. We may also have placed higher expectations on ourselves.

Self-esteem and self-confidence, the focuses of this chapter, can either be strengthened or broken down over time. In Chapter 3, you learned how to change your thoughts and your standard mode using anchor thoughts, visualization, winning morning rituals, and collecting gold nuggets. Now, you will learn how to build up your self-esteem and self-confidence, which requires determined action. It's important that we control our thoughts and say good things about ourselves, but it's just as important that we do good things for ourselves and live by our own code of honor. We're going to let go of the brake and start driving.

SELF-ESTEEM AND SELF-CONFIDENCE

Self-esteem is how much you appreciate and like yourself, that is, your own self-image. Self-esteem is a deep conviction that you are worthy. Self-confidence is a feeling that you are capable, confident in your abilities and your capacity to handle the challenges you face. Self-confidence is not just the belief that you can fix things and handle situations; it's just as much about being able to handle uncertainty and not knowing the outcome but daring to do it anyway. To trust yourself, even when you don't know how to do it.

When I started therapy, I thought self-esteem was a vague concept. It wasn't enough that I told myself I was capable and a good person. I still doubted my own worth. I didn't realize at the time that action was at least as important as the things that I told myself. I didn't understand that self-esteem and self-confidence are like siblings; they belong together and give the most effect when they cooperate. If you work on your self-esteem, you will affect your self-confidence as well, and vice versa. In my work as a coach, I notice my clients often don't know how to strengthen their self-esteem or self-confidence, and they often say, "It doesn't help that I tell myself I'm good enough because I can't feel it. I don't believe it." To believe and feel you are capable and you have the capacity to grow, you need to experience it in practice. It's also good to know the following when it comes to self-esteem and self-confidence:

- Self-esteem and self-confidence are not static. Self-esteem isn't high or low. Self-confidence is not good or bad. Instead, they fluctuate from day to day, hour to hour. But you can build a solid foundation where self-esteem and self-confidence are more robust.

- Self-esteem or self-confidence isn't something that you either have or don't have. It's something you build up and then constantly exercise, just like with your physical fitness. You can't go for a run once a year and expect yourself to be in good shape. You also can't make sporadic attempts to strengthen self-esteem or self-confidence; you need to exercise them regularly. You can train them, just like muscles, regardless of your starting point.

- Self-confidence can be patchy. You trust yourself and your abilities in some areas and in certain situations but not in others. You will not have the same confidence in all areas. In areas in which you have more experience or more victories, you will naturally have stronger self-confidence.

- The seeds of a low self-esteem and self-confidence can be sown in childhood, through experiences that have made us doubt our own worth or our abilities. Self-esteem and self-confidence then tend to weaken over time if we do not train these muscles.

CLIENT STORY

Not Now

Mats came to me because he wanted to work on his low self-esteem. Mats had a hard time saying no, he compared himself to others, and he often felt like "a loser." He felt blue and had begun to lose the joy of life. His low self-esteem stemmed from his early childhood. Mats loved and admired his dad. Every day, when his dad came home, Mats rushed into the hallway, eager to have a moment with his dad and show him what he had done during the day. The little boy was usually met by a tired dad who said,

"Not now." His dad then settled down in front of the TV and disappeared into his own world. Mats often sat waiting for the time to be "now," but "now" usually didn't come. As time went on, Mats stopped running into the hallway to meet his dad. When I asked Mats how that felt, he told me it made him sad and admitted, "It felt like I wasn't important." This interpretation became Mats's default mode, and he felt unimportant even as an adult. The interpretation became a belief that prevailed until we reprogrammed it.

In this example we can see how an interpretation can cause problems. As an adult, you can understand that dad is tired after working, which he does every day to provide for his family. A small child cannot make this interpretation. To develop a good self-esteem, a child needs to be treated as a valuable person whose needs are important. So, don't forget to give your children lots of love, encouragement, and attention.

NOTHING IS IMPOSSIBLE

When we are children, we believe everything is possible. We dare to venture into an unknown world to explore it, with curiosity and courage. When does this "nothing is impossible" attitude disappear?

When you are seventeen years old, you have heard the word *no* about 150,000 times, and the word *yes* only 5,000 times. When you are told what you can or can't do, have or can't have, or who you can or can't become, a neurological highway is eventually created in the brain, and it can be difficult to change. When someone is constantly pointing out what you did wrong or what you could have done better, you start to doubt your own abilities. When you can't do things right or understand things, when you can't mediate between your parents when they're fighting, when you can't make your mom happy, when you can't fall asleep when you are supposed to, and when you have an older sibling you never can trump, you start to doubt your abilities. The evidence is overwhelming: I can't do it! You begin to feel helpless and powerless. Your POWER disappears.

Children don't yet understand they aren't supposed to be able to handle some situations; instead, they think that they are bad or incapable or the problem is impossible to solve. We become world champions in giving up. Often, we give up before we have even tried. Even when we are adults.

Many people believe they completely lack confidence because they have been dumped, failed at certain tasks, lost competitions, failed to get a job, or have been reminded that they are insufficient in some other way. In these cases, we tend to create a global fact—I lack self-confidence. This isn't true. Nobody lacks self-confidence in all areas. If you didn't have any self-confidence, you wouldn't have gotten out of bed in the morning. Self-confidence is just faltering in some areas. If we repeatedly tell ourselves we are a person with poor self-confidence, this will create an identity. We will believe that "this is the way I am." This ultimately affects all areas of our lives. We become what we think we are.

Children depend on their parents to survive. When we were small, we needed them to help us with just about everything. Sometimes, that belief can follow us into adulthood. Someone else should make sure our needs are met. Our employers, our children, our friends, our partners. *They* will make us happy. *They* will take care of us. We simply use the same programming we did when we were young children. We forget that now that we are adults, we can actually take care of ourselves and learn new skills, which seemed impossible before we did it for the first time. When you were a kid, you decided to start walking. You got up, fell, got up, fell, got up, walked a few steps, and fell. You kept trying until you could walk steadily. You had no voice inside that said, "It's not worth it. I can't do it. It's not possible." If that voice had existed, a lot of people would still be crawling. You can accomplish most of what you set your mind on.

Learning new things can sometimes feel overwhelming and create that feeling that you won't succeed. Writing this book has, at times, felt overwhelming to me. I didn't really know if I would be able to do it, or if anyone would be interested in reading it, because I think what I'm saying has already been said by others. Some things are new and thus a little more difficult. Feeling insecure at first is part of the process. Some things are easier for us because we have done them before, we have succeeded before, and we have a lot of experience. Feeling nervous, overwhelmed, or insecure doesn't mean there is something wrong with us; it only means we are going somewhere new, where we don't have as much experience, or where we have experienced a set-back or two. When we build our confidence, we will move forward, fall, get up, and move forward again. Just like when we learned how to walk.

SELF-DOUBT CAN START EARLY

As a fetus, we respond to our mother's environment. We don't have direct access to the surroundings outside our mother but can sense her emotions. Did you know that a fetus can adjust its biology and behavior to adapt to the mother's experience of the environment? The reason is that when the baby is born, she or he will live in the same environment as the mother. The fetus picks up information about the external environment via the placenta. It was previously believed the placenta provided only physical nutrition, but it also provides information. Molecules and hormones found in the mother's blood carry information, which is communicated to the fetus. So, what affects the mother emotionally also affects the fetus. For example, if the mother experiences fear, these hormones flow into the fetus and the fetus learns the world out there isn't safe. The fetus obviously has no words to describe it. Instead, it is an experienced belief, a structural part of the fetal mind during development. We are not born as a clean slate but with programmed information. Researchers call this the preverbal memory. David is an interesting example of how beliefs seem to form as early as during the fetal period.

CLIENT STORY

Where's the Exit?

David had loved film his whole life. After working on several smaller films, he had the chance of a lifetime to go to the United States, but he was hesitant. He was scared of not succeeding and having to leave the film industry with his tail between his legs. He wanted to seize the opportunity, but at the same time, he was constantly worried about how things would go and couldn't view the possibilities in a positive light. After some follow-up questions, we discovered he often backed down when it came to new challenges. He tended to choose the safe path or became passive and followed the advice of others, rather than listening to himself. But he wanted to take on the challenge of moving to Hollywood. "This is a chance you only get once in your life," he explained.

During the session, David had the feeling of being drugged, disoriented, scared, and without power. As we followed the emotion back in time, he found deep, buried momentary sensations from the time he was in his mother's womb. He knew that his birth had been painful for his mother and that she had been given wrongly-dosed epidural anesthesia. David told me he was feeling numb and didn't know how to get out.

We all have preverbal memories. They are neither verbal nor stored as images. Instead, they are saved as implicit memories or, so-called body memories. Psychologist Arthur Janov believes that a traumatic birth can remain as an imprint in our nervous system, even into adulthood. These memories or imprints can be triggered when we become scared or stressed, no matter how old we are.

Fetuses normally know how to get out through the birth canal; it's encoded in them. Most of the time, the fetus moves around to find the best and easiest way to squeeze out. This is their first challenge. When David was helped out by the doctors, the first seed of self-doubt was sown, the feeling that he couldn't cope with challenges. The feeling of not being able to rely on his ability grew ever stronger over the years.

I loved the email I received six months later. "I am no longer afraid of challenges. I feel that I can trust myself and my own ability. I can do anything. I can handle everything. It feels fantastic." This is a clear example of what can happen when we break away from a limiting label.

Many researchers believe early memories are not reliable and rarely represent an exact replay of the original event, due to the memory system being malleable. Our memories can be fragmented and disorganized, and the earliest memories are often just feelings or summations of the original experience, without much detail. Is David's memory true? I don't know, but if a problem he has experienced throughout his adult life is gone, I'm satisfied. If we solve it in one session, I'm more than happy.

David's story shows that your self-confidence and a belief in your own ability can be dislocated by just about anything. You don't need to have mean parents or a bad upbringing. And if you are a parent, try to stop worrying about how you are affecting your children because no matter what you do, you will never be perfect.

 ## YODA MOMENT
Questions About Your Self-Esteem

What happened in your life that made you feel unimportant and less valuable?

- How did your parents treat you? Did they see you, did they listen to you, did they respect your boundaries, and did they praise you?
- Did your parents often prioritize something else? Their jobs, their own needs, another sibling, the TV, or their mobile phones?
- Did your parents show emotions and tell you they loved you?
- Did you often feel like you were in their way, a burden, or that you could never do anything right?
- Did your parents often get angry or disappointed in you?
- In what ways are you still hard on yourself?

Reflect and write down in your journal.

Questions About Your Self-Confidence

What events in your life have made you doubt your own abilities and created a feeling that you're not capable?

- When you did something, did your parents praise you or look for mistakes?
- Was it reasonable for you handle the things that were expected of you?

- Did you often hear you were wrong or that you should know better?
- Did your parents or other adults get angry with you when you did something wrong?
- Did you feel that adults were disappointed in your efforts?
- Did your parents encourage you to try things yourself, or did they help you with everything?
- Did you experience competition with siblings or friends?
- Did you think you should have done better? Did you feel that you failed with something as a child?
- Were there situations when you didn't know how to do something and didn't receive any guidance?

Make a list of areas or situations where you have good self-confidence and another with areas where you have less self-confidence. It gives clarity on where you really stand, and you can see more clearly that self-confidence is patchy.

Before we go through the practical steps on how to build up both self-esteem and self-confidence, it's good to take a quick look at what can be part of good self-esteem and good self-confidence.

Good Self-Esteem

- You stand up for yourself and set boundaries.
- You dare to express your needs and opinions.
- You can make your own decisions.
- You can say no.
- You respect yourself.
- You feel safe in many situations.
- You feel equal to others.
- You accept and display many different emotions.
- You are proud of yourself.
- You can appreciate yourself and others.
- You can see your own and others' strengths and weaknesses and accept them.
- You like to grow and to find meaning with life.
- You have a positive outlook on life.

- You invite people into your life.
- You have clarified your values and live by them.
- You want to make a difference.
- You have a good balance between work, leisure, and relaxation.
- You dare to take on challenges and take risks to grow. You learn from your mistakes.
- You can receive feedback and criticism without taking it personally.
- You are in your power and will not be manipulated.
- You can receive praise.
- You dare to be genuine.

Good Self-Confidence

- You have confidence in your own ability to meet challenges, solve problems, and deal with different situations and people.
- You have the ability to handle the unknown.
- You trust your own judgment of people and situations.
- You know you can influence people and situations.

As you notice, there are more items regarding self-esteem. There is nothing wrong with that. Self-confidence is more straightforward, while self-esteem has more nuances.

Some of the points above may feel open-and-shut to you, and there are probably areas where you feel more insecure and that need to be strengthened. If you find it difficult to succeed with some of the points, it's because you lack experience. You simply haven't learned what to do yet, or you have failed in the past and think you can't do it now either. With the right knowledge and training, you will succeed. Whether it's talking to people, studying at the university, asking someone you like on a date, making your own decisions, winning a contest, or setting boundaries.

⚙ JEDI MIND TRICKS

Now, we will move on to the practical steps. Strong self-confidence is not a personality trait. You don't have to believe in yourself. You just have to try. "Over and over and over." It's a journey, not something that happens overnight. Trying new things and coping with them builds self-confidence. However, staying in your comfort zone can lower your self-confidence. You won't grow as a person, and therefore, you won't experience the feeling of mastering things. When you challenge yourself and manage new things, you will grow as a person. You will be proud of yourself, and that's an important cornerstone of a good self-esteem. Just as I mentioned before, self-confidence and self-esteem go hand in hand. I know you can do this, just like I see the progress of my clients on a daily basis.

The most common excuses my clients use for not letting go of the brake and taking active steps to build their self-esteem and self-confidence are: it's hard, uncomfortable, scary, they can't do it, they are afraid, and it's impossible. Many people think they should feel valuable, strong, courageous, ready, and motivated before they act. It's quite the opposite. When you act, you will build your value and your strength. You will become braver and more ready the more you exercise. When you see what you have already done, the motivation kicks in. So, you shouldn't wait for the right time; you have to let go of the brake and move forward.

No one is asking you to stand up to the most frightening person in your life right away or to speak in front of a group of people within a week. You start with small steps. Just like when you exercise, you start with the lightest weights. In front of whom, or in what situation, can you be more courageous right now? It doesn't have to be a conflict. It may be enough to make your voice heard at work when you decide where to have lunch—that you don't automatically answer that it doesn't matter when someone asks you what you want, that you tell the massage therapist how you want to be massaged, or say that you have an idea during a meeting. Start with positive contexts. When you are ready, you increase the difficulty level. From saying what you think is great, what you like and want, you can start to say what you don't like and share your opinion when you're not quite sure how the surroundings will react. Finally, you can speak your mind during conflicts, say STOP, and stand up to people who don't treat you with respect. You have your whole life to improve, so take one step at a time. But you need to start taking action.

Here come the Jedi Mind Tricks that will make you an action hero in your own life.

O—ᴛ HACK #6

THE 5-SECOND RULE

One myth that needs to be crushed is that before you can start moving forward you must have motivation, courage, confidence, or direction. We have bought into the idea that we must feel ready for change. That we should wake up one day and feel motivated, brave, have the confidence, and know where we're going. We're waiting for the right time. The problem is that our brains are not designed to do things that are new, difficult, scary, or uncomfortable. They are designed to keep us safe, save energy, and ensure our survival. To grow, develop, follow dreams, change jobs, or enter into a relationship, we need to do things that are new, difficult, scary or uncomfortable.

We will rarely feel like taking challenging steps because our brains hit the brakes. Usually, the brake is subtly activated. We hesitate. We sit in a meeting and want to contribute with an idea, but instead of sharing the idea, we hesitate and stop ourselves. We want to approach a person who seems exciting, but instead of doing so, we hesitate and go to the bar. What we don't understand is that when we hesitate, during that microsecond, a stress signal is sent to the brain that puts it on alert: Why are you hesitating? Something must be going on. Is something wrong? The brain is now starting to protect you in millions of ways. One of the brain's favorite methods to protect you is to keep you inside your head and make you think. You doubt, analyze, and then never take action. Your anxiety, nervousness, insecurity, or fear has hijacked you.

When we were younger, we usually had someone encouraging us. I remember how my dad playfully pushed me into the water when we went swimming. Without that push, I probably wouldn't have gotten into the water because I was a bath coward. As adults, we must push ourselves and stop hesitating so often. As we move forward, we experience pride, which also strengthens our self-esteem. For each step we take, we prove to ourselves that we can do it, and our confidence is strengthened.

Research shows that you have a small window of opportunity where you can take control of yourself and make a decision to act before the brain cuts you off. This window is open for about five seconds and based on this concept, the best-selling author and TV personality, Mel Robbins, created the "5-Second Rule."

Every time you do something that feels uncomfortable, scary, difficult, or new, count down from five to one, as if you were counting down to a rocket launch. 5-4-3-2-1-GO! On the word "go," activate the body through some form of movement. Counting down along with the body movement breaks your thought loop. It's a ritual that will help you stop thinking and instead, start acting. It disables your autopilot and awakens your prefrontal cortex, your chief executive, which turns on the drive. You simply get out of your brain.

Let's take one example. It is morning; you sit on your bedside and look out the window. It is dark and the rain is pouring down. You have decided to walk thirty minutes each morning. You start to think about whether you should drink your coffee first or respond to some emails. Or you feel that you probably have a pain in your knee.

Suddenly, thirty minutes have passed, and you no longer have time for your morning walk before work. Your brain has hijacked you, and the brake is set. You can't hesitate for many seconds because then the game is lost. Push yourself up with a 5-4-3-2-1-GO, walk firmly out into the hall, put on your outerwear, and head out.

As early as the nineteenth century, the Swedish scientist Svante Arrhenius understood that the most difficult thing is to do is start something. A large amount of activation energy is required to create a spark that starts a chain reaction—much like some people need their cup of coffee in the morning to get started. The 5-Second Rule is a way of generating activation energy. The countdown awakens the part of the brain that you need to get started. Once you have started, it's easier to continue.

There's also a biological reason as to why we sometimes find it difficult to get out of our comfort zones. In the past, few people traveled more than a few miles from their birthplace. Those who were rebellious and adventurous left, often without returning. It's risky and sometimes lonely to be a rebel. In addition, independent people have always been dangerous to the established order in society; and therefore, you, as a rebel, can be quite stubbornly opposed.

The best thing about the 5-Second Rule is that it can be used for just about anything. As soon as you have an instinct to act toward your goals, and if you tend to hesitate, count 5-4-3-2-1-GO, let go of the brake, and move. Share an idea at a meeting, approach a person and introduce yourself, get out of bed, sign up for a course, clean out a storage room, sort out a misunderstanding . . . the list goes on. Of course, you count quietly in your head. You don't want to sound like a complete lunatic. And don't forget that on "go," you activate the body.

Write a list of five things you want to do this month. Clean up? Start? Quit? Meet? Clear up? Challenge yourself and don't pick only easy things. Choose some easier and some more difficult assignments. Some things you may be able to both begin and end this month; others may become part of your everyday life.

O⇀ HACK #7

STOP COMPLAINING

We have a tendency to complain about everything. The complaining is a habit we have created. In the end, it becomes so familiar that it becomes invisible. Whining about things isn't observing what is happening; it is a conscious choice to zoom in on the bad things. When you constantly express your displeasure, you reinforce your negative default mode. The more you complain, the more negative energy you store, and the more you attract what you are unhappy with.

Why are we complaining?

- To avoid doing anything. The whining gives us an excuse to postpone activities and goals. It's easier to complain than do something.
- To avoid responsibility. For example, if you constantly arrive late for work and blame the traffic, you may want to consider leaving home earlier. Complaining to others can also be a way to avoid responsibility. Others are wrong, others should change, and we're the victims.
- To gain attention and confirm beliefs.
- To create community, we complain together.
- Because we are bored and the whining creates drama—something happens.
- To gain power over others.
- To excuse ourselves for not reaching a certain standard (I was blinded by the sun).

- Because we fear that if we aren't dissatisfied, we will stop striving. To complain and be dissatisfied is one way to push ourselves forward in life. In my opinion, it's better to be driven by curiosity, energy, and joy.

It's good to have a balance between acceptance and taking responsibility. Many of us complain about things we can't change. The weather, traffic or another person's faults. Acceptance is better here. In other situations, we should inform when something is wrong so it can be corrected. But stick to the facts. Taking responsibility means that you become aware that you are complaining and either stop complaining, look for solutions, or leave the situation. Accountability requires courage, which you can strengthen.

 Consider if there is something else you're dissatisfied with as you direct your dissatisfaction elsewhere. For example, on your partner, the woman in the checkout line, or the bus that is delayed.

O—⊓ HACK #8

FOLLOW YOUR CODE OF HONOR

The Ten Commandments were a kind of code of honor. In ancient Egypt, there were actually forty-two commandments, moral cosmic laws everyone was supposed to follow. The people were expected to act truthfully and with honor in all situations that affected the family, society, the land, and the gods. After a person's death, the soul's heart was weighed against the feather of truth, where one's actions were judged by, among others, the goddess Ma'at, who represented truth, justice, order, and morality. If you followed the laws, you gained access to Osiris's paradise.

Our code of honor is like a list of commandments, a moral code with values we need to follow to feel like a good person. Acting with integrity is important for us to feel proud of ourselves and respect ourselves. Pride and self-respect are two important cornerstones of self-esteem. When we break our code of honor, we can erode our self-esteem.

Think about what code of honor you have and if you live by it as much as you can? Create your own internal sense of what you define as a wise and good person. The most important thing is that you feel you have done what is right, according to *your* values. This is when you can stand strong and be proud of yourself, even though others may think you should have done more, less, or something different.

Here are some examples of "commandments" that can be included in a code of honor:

Tell the Truth

Every now and then, most of us lie about ourselves, to ourselves, and to others. This reinforces our outward masks; we don't show our true selves. Lies ultimately make us not know who we are anymore.

Self-esteem is not only about what you think and feel about yourself but also about knowing yourself. Knowing who you are, what you stand for, and what you want. To know those things, you must begin to tell the truth . . . both to yourself, about yourself, and to others. "The truth will set you free" is a telling quote. When you are true to yourself, you become free to be who you are. Not just the version you created to fit into the world, but who you really are, beyond the programming—your matrix. "Welcome to the real world," as Morpheus says in the movie *The Matrix*.

Telling the truth is also important for us to be proud of ourselves. When we don't tell the truth, we break our code of honor, becoming liars, and self-esteem is eroded. To make us feel better, we often create a subcategory of lies—white lies. We can lie to make it easier for us, to protect ourselves, or to avoid hurting others. The problem with the white lie is that it is still a lie and can erode our pride and self-respect, even if it's small. Some lies may slip through, but if they become too many, our self-esteem will be adversely affected.

How do you become honest?

A good step can be to not always automatically reply "everything is good" when someone asks you how you feel. Start saying how you feel, for real. It doesn't have to be a long exposition; a short answer is enough. Another step may be to be honest when you don't have the energy or desire to meet someone. Often, we come up with excuses, such as having to take care of the children, do homework,

work, or fix the car, and then we lie down on the sofa and watch Netflix. We don't want to disappoint the other person, and we're scared of being judged, so we come up with a rational explanation that sounds better than saying that we want to lie on the sofa.

Be honest. Show that the person is important to you by booking a meeting later. If the person is disappointed, accept it. Maybe even see it as a compliment. The person had been looking forward to meeting you, which means you are important to them.

Speaking the truth will sometimes be a bit scary. People will be angry, annoyed, and disappointed. Some may not understand you or refuse to comply. But if you want to maintain self-respect and self-esteem, be authentic and genuine. You need to be honest. Start small. How can you be more authentic and honest with who you are?

I'm still working on being more honest with myself and others. Sometimes, it's easy; sometimes, the fear flutters in my stomach; and sometimes, the fear paralyzes my entire body. However, I strive on, and every time I choose to be honest, it becomes easier, and I feel proud of myself.

Being Honest with Yourself

Sometimes we have been dishonest for such a long time that we no longer have a clue about who we really are. Many clients come to me with a desire to get to know themselves and discover what they want. They hope to find their passion, purpose, and joy. Addressing these big issues can seem overwhelming, but it doesn't have to be that way. Honesty is the first step to finding your inner home. Then you will find your passion, purpose, and joy.

Use your scouting skills and discover where you can be more honest, both with yourself and others. Remember, being honest doesn't mean being brutal or mean.

Keep Your Promises

Not keeping promises to yourself or others is also a way to erode your integrity and, thus, your self-esteem. The more often you break promises, the less your promises are worth. You lose power and creativity because there is no implementation that backs up your words. There is no walking the talk. It also becomes harder to like yourself because we generally find it difficult to like people who break promises. For example, if you decide to walk thirty minutes each day but don't, you will probably get angry with and disappointed in yourself for not doing what you said. Your inner judgment is eroding your self-esteem.

Become your own scout and notice how often you break promises. Can you be more vigilant about what you promise, and not promise things you can't keep or do?

Stop Taking Part in Negative Gossip

When you gossip, an unpleasant residue is left in your energy system. Residues of negativity and judgment block your energy. If you can't or don't dare to say your opinion directly to the person, try to keep quiet. Talking derisively about someone else lowers you because most of us don't like a gossiper.

Do It Again and Do It Right

Have you treated someone in a way that isn't in line with your code of honor? Unfortunately, it may remain in your energy system until you have resolved it. I have worked with clients who have felt bad for ten, twenty, and even forty years because they stole money from their mom's wallet to buy candy, beat a friend in school, or lied to their best friend. We will make lots of mistakes; it's part of being human, but we can often correct what we have done wrong.

Make a list of what or whom you need to make amends with. Do you feel guilty when you think about the event or person? Take a deep breath and start crossing off the list.

Do Good, Become Good

This idea goes back to Aristotle. You can't just imagine change. To become a more positive, happier person, you need to do something in practice. When you do something good, it gives you the feeling that you're a good person. A person who does good is usually happier. Donate time to help someone, call and ask how a friend is doing, do a neighbor a favor, or hold the door for a stranger. Small everyday acts of kindness will create pride and joy inside you.

Stand in Your Own Ring Corner

Standing up for yourself and possibly making someone else angry or disappointed isn't always easy, but with practice, it's not only possible but worth it. When you stand in your own ring corner, you prove to yourself that you are valuable and your self-esteem increases. Here are some tips on how to stand up for yourself in a respectful way:

- **Buy yourself time.** When someone asks for your help, there are two things you can do. First of all, before you answer that you can help, take some time to think about the consequences of your answer. Ask to get back to them; say that you need to sleep on it or that you need to talk with someone before you can say yes (even if this someone is yourself). Secondly, tell the person that you may not be able to help them. For example, you might say that you have just made a decision to limit your commitments. If you prepare people at an early stage that you may not be able to help them, their disappointment will not be as great, and you will give them the chance to consider other opportunities. This was something I practiced extensively for a period. I asked to get back to people. In the beginning, it took a long time for me to decide what I wanted, sometimes several weeks. After a while, I could reduce the decision time to a weekend or just sleep on it. Today, I can usually say no right away. If a situation arises today where I falter and find it difficult to say no or decide, I ask for a couple of days to reflect.

- **Check your gut feeling.** Once you have bought yourself time, the next step is to check your gut feeling and ask yourself if what someone is asking you to do is really something you want to do. On a scale of one to ten, how much do you want to do it? If you can't decide, you might ask yourself, "If I knew the person wouldn't get angry, disappointed, or upset, would I say no then?" In the beginning, it's easy to get worried about how others will react, but you need to dare to be true to yourself. And of course, you will sometimes do things that you don't like, but you do them because they are important to someone you care about. You can do things to show love and strengthen the relationship, not on the basis of guilt or out of duty.

- **Tell the truth with kindness.** When we find it difficult to disappoint others or to say no, it's often because we don't really know how to express ourselves in a good way. Be honest and let the person know that you are sorry you need to say no. The important thing is not to leave room for persuasion. Don't be unclear by saying that you don't think you can help, but if something changes you might be able to. Be kind, but do not give the impression that you are open to discussion. Tell the truth directly, simply, and in a straight-forward manner.

O⚊ᴛ HACK #9

BE GENEROUS WITH PRAISE

When we have low self-esteem, we often seek praise and affirmation from others to feel valuable. We become people pleasers. The need for confirmation is growing because we're not fueling ourselves, and we must then be refilled through others. When our internal account is empty, we can start doing pretty extreme things to get refilled. We can become confirmation junkies, totally dependent on external praise. However, it doesn't help when others fill up our account balance; we need to do it ourselves. It's our own praise that nourishes us in the long run and in a deeper way. Other's confirmation is the icing on the cake, but it can never be the cake itself.

Why are we so dependent on external confirmation? When we were little, our whole value system and existence depended on our parents' approval. Seeking their affirmation in order to receive love, community, and security became the most important avenue for us. If we spent much of our childhood satisfying our parents, there is a risk we will also spend a large portion of our adult life trying to please others. We sometimes think we need the approval of others to succeed. Of course, we cannot be completely independent of the approval of others. Sometimes, we need to prove ourselves worthy of a specific job, a certain salary, area of responsibility, or a home mortgage.

Praise Yourself

All praise shouldn't derive from your actions. If it does, the interpretation becomes: if you do good things, you're good. If you make a mistake or act incorrectly, you're bad. Every time you fail to meet the standard of the person who rewards you, whether that's yourself or someone else, you believe you have failed and are filled with guilt. Instead, praise yourself for who you are. A good person, caring, helpful, positive, honest, responsible, happy, funny . . . fill in the adjectives that fit you. Regularly praising yourself affects your positive standard mode. What you tell yourself determines everything. When you are empathetic to yourself, it's much easier to succeed than if you complain at yourself. When you criticize yourself, you will eventually crush all motivation. We are not particularly motivated or inspired to do things when someone is putting us down. It doesn't matter if the criticism comes from outside or from within.

Praise the Right Thing

When you praise what you do, praise your efforts, not the results, because you can't always influence the outcome. If you praise what you can influence—your efforts and your commitment—your brain will want to put more effort into it next time. Studies show that we are more likely to invest if we believe it's possible to reach the goal and if we allow the brain to experience progress. Therefore, focus on what you have already achieved, not just on what you haven't done yet.

Make a list of everything you have already accomplished and read it several times. Divide your missions into several smaller goals so that the brain experiences multiple small victories. This makes it motivated to continue. The brain loves the experience of progress, and it creates a craving for more. If we celebrate our success during the journey, we encourage the brain to continue. Regularly check on what you have accomplished. Every night, write down something you are proud of, something you did, and something you accomplished. Collect your gold nuggets as you learned in Chapter 3. If it feels strange to praise yourself, imagine giving the praise to a toddler. Your inner child. I like to think of my inner little girl when I give myself praise. I can see and feel how happy it makes her.

O⇉ HACK #10

LEAVE THE MIDDLE LINE

In school, the focus is often placed on what we need to become better at instead of focusing more on what we're already good at and making sure we become super good at it. If we are bad at math, we need to study more math to get better grades. The subjects we're already good at or enjoy, we seldom get to practice. This means, as adults, we're staying in the middle. We know a little about everything, but we have rarely had the opportunity to engage in a special interest that could become our greatest success. When we focus too much on what we're less successful at, we lower our self-confidence. Therefore, don't spend all your time working on your weaknesses. Focus on your strengths. Be amazing at what you're good at and like to do. If you don't think you're good at anything, think again. There's always something you're good at or think is fun. When something is fun to do, there's a great chance that you will end up being good at it as well.

Identify your strengths. What can you do to further strengthen these? What are you good at that you can do more of?

CHAPTER 4 IN 60 SECONDS

- Good self-esteem and self-confidence are something you build up and constantly exercise, just as with your physical fitness.
- Self-confidence is patchy. You trust yourself and your ability in some areas and certain situations but not in others.
- Create an internal sense of what you define as a wise and good person.
- **The 5-Second Rule.** When you have an instinct to act toward a goal or when you hesitate, count 5-4-3-2-1-GO. Let go of the brake and move.
- **Stop complaining.** To complain isn't to observe what is happening, it's a choice to zoom in on the bad things. Complaining reinforces your negative default mode.
- **Follow your code of honor.** Following your moral code is important to feel proud of yourself. Pride strengthens your self-esteem.
- **Be generous with praise.** Praise yourself for who you are and for your efforts. The most important praise is your own. Another's praise is the icing on the cake.
- **Leave the middle line.** Focus on your strengths and do more of what you're good at.

CHAPTER 5

SUFFERING FROM EMOTIONAL CRAMP?

Emotions are energy in motion. They need to be released.
Suppressed emotions are stacked on top of each other and
eventually come out, regardless of situation, recipient, or cost.

He squeezes the end of the toothpaste tube. She squeezes the middle. The irritation is growing. One day, he can no longer hold back. "You are supposed to squeeze the end of the tube! Everyone knows that," he says, annoyed. She thinks he's exaggerating. The fight is on.

But is it really about the toothpaste tube? Probably not. Instead, minor annoyances tend to be about something completely different. The toothpaste tube becomes the trigger for an underlying frustration to erupt.

It is common for us to hold on to our feelings because we don't want to, or are unable to, express them in certain situations or in front of certain people. The hidden feelings then explode elsewhere. For example, in the bathroom, when it is time for tooth brushing, or when we come home after a bad day at work and step on one of the children's Lego pieces in the hall. "How many times have I told you to pick up your Lego pieces when you're done playing?" The scolding becomes a bit too harsh because we carry a lot of trapped feelings from earlier in the day. We are suffering from emotional cramp.

EMOTIONS AND FEELINGS

Let me start by explaining the difference between emotions and feelings. During an event, we experience physical sensations in the body. Biochemical reactions are created, which causes the body to react. Emotions are the body's reaction to an event and come before the feelings. Emotional reactions are stored as memories in the body, and since long ago, these have served the function of saving us from dangerous situations and helping us find what makes us feel good. Our emotions are instinctive, temporary, and when not activated, they rest deep in our subconscious.

When we give the physical sensations, our emotions, a label, they become feelings. Simply put, one can say that feelings are a mental reaction to emotions; they are the brain's interpretation of an emotional event. The brain summarizes all of the information that comes from the body's systems—the immune system, the nervous system, and the endocrine system (the hormone system)—and then interprets the information as a feeling. Feelings are subjective and arise from the experiences, memories, and beliefs we have accumulated during our lifetimes.

Emotions and feelings play a significant role in our lives. Feelings are the driving force behind our behavior, whether positive or negative. Since most of us are unaware of how our emotions and feelings control our lives, we don't always understand why we react the way we do in certain situations. To make it easier, I will use the word feelings in the future as I describe how we emotionally experience things.

ARE YOU SUFFERING FROM EMOTIONAL CRAMP?

Feelings/emotions are energy in motion. The goal is that feelings, just like food, should move through the body and then out. If your food doesn't come out but gets stuck in the intestines, you get a stomach cramp. If you keep negative emotions in the body, you get an emotional cramp. The purpose of feelings is that, just like with our children, we should experience them fully and then let go of them. If we push them down, we create a ticking bomb with stagnant energy. The feelings get stuck in the body. They are stacked on top of each other, and eventually, they come out, regardless of the situation, recipient, or cost. We get easily stressed, upset, angry, or on edge. Supressed feelings can lead to anger, depression, a sense of hopelessness, sadness, and panic anxiety.

Few of us actually express our feelings to the full extent. We push our feelings under the surface and distract or numb them with other things; for example, food, drugs, alcohol, sex, work, exercise, or shopping. But it's like trying to push a beach ball under the water—the ball will always pop up to the surface again.

Children are usually better at expressing their feelings directly; and therefore, their emotional outbursts pass faster. But after many wrinkled eyebrows and admonitions to behave "correctly," children begin to suppress their feelings under the surface. Unfortunately, we can only push the emotions below the surface for a while before they create an emotional mountain inside us.

Studies show that if we avoid or suppress our feelings, we strengthen them, and then, more of our energy supply is needed to keep them in place. Many clients tell me how their energy came back when they let go of old feelings. If the feelings are pushed down for too long, they can manifest physically. John E. Sarno, a professor of rehabilitation medicine, appointed America's best physician by *Forbes Magazine*, believes physical pain is often rooted in our mental and emotional life. Unexpressed feelings and fears create chronic tension, which in turn, leads to physical pain. I can see this very clearly in some of my clients. Years of fear, sadness, anger, frustration, and worry create a stressed nervous system and a tense body. Finally, physical pain occurs. Sarno has even found that chronic pain often acts as a protective mechanism, a distraction from feelings that we are not ready to face. We focus so much on the physical pain that we forget what we really need to work on.

FOOLHARDY ADVENTURES

I have been really good at pushing down my feelings. My dad hated weakness and being emotional was a sign of this. He wanted to show his strength to everyone and often did so through impulsive and sometimes daring actions. He liked adventure. He would swim as far out into the sea as he could, with me in tow in a small inflatable plastic boat. Or he would go climbing in the Alps and let me dangle off the cliff edge holding on to only his hand. My dad was my biggest idol, and I wanted to be just like him, so I proved my strength by never expressing my fear. I pushed down my fear for many years, until it became so big that I couldn't hold it under the surface any longer. Fear began to emerge in all possible contexts. It was only when I dared to let go of the fear and set limits on what was okay or not okay for me that the fear began to fade away. I sorted out which fears were realistic to keep because they were there to protect me and which fears I could let go of. I had to teach myself to dare to be vulnerable and human.

CLIENT STORY

We Just Want Out

As a child, Camilla had many feelings and was considered sensitive and temperamental. None of Camilla's parents showed much emotion, and her father often told her she was hypersensitive and shouldn't cry over small things. Camilla's father also became angry with her when she showed her willpower, especially when she was a toddler. She often had to go into her room and "think about" what she had done. Camilla felt lonely and misunderstood. To gain the approval and love of her parents, she shut down her feelings and mimicked her parents. When she was compliant, she was rewarded. But beneath the surface, all of the old feelings were stacking up. In adulthood, Camilla suffered from severe anxiety. Sometimes, the emotions came out in the form of dramatic, emotional outbursts.

When Camilla came to me, she wanted to experience a more balanced life and be free of her anxiety. Quite quickly, we found the cause of the emotional outbursts and anxiety—the old feelings that were trapped and wanted out. Remember: Emotions are energy in motion. When we lock them in, they become like caged animals. Together, we helped the little girl who had shut down her feelings to both feel and express them again. The little girl got an okay to be herself, accepting all sides of her personality. After a few sessions and homework to feel and express her feelings and needs in different situations, the anxiety and outbursts subsides.

After six months, Camilla was in balance, and the anxiety attacks had completely disappeared. She also found more of her POWER, the power she had as a two- and three-year-old, before her willpower was suffocated. When Camilla allowed the power to come out and move freely, she became more creative, got things done, and what she wanted in life began to manifest.

THE BODY IS LIVING IN THE WRONG AGE

The subconscious has no idea of time and space; therefore, we can hold onto thoughts, feelings, and behaviors for many years. The subconscious is fully convinced the rules that were set when you were five years old still apply. The subconscious has no idea that many years have passed and that an update of your thoughts, feelings, behaviors, rules, and beliefs might have occurred. Therefore, in some situations, you can still respond as a five-year-old, even though you are in your thirties, forties, or fifties.

The body also lives in the past. It stores what we experienced for a long time. Stored feelings are like chemical archives of past experiences and can be activated by our thoughts, among other things. Let's say your dad got angry and scolded you when you did something wrong. You got scared and started shaking. As an adult, when you have a male manager with a hot temperament who calls you into his office, you unknowingly activate the same emotional chemicals as when you were a child. You feel scared and start shaking. When you come home and tell your partner about your experience, you produce the same emotional chemicals again. When you think about the incident with your boss a month later, the same thing happens. You live in your old memories. You cannot move forward when the feelings are still in the present. In addition, if you repeat the event, you bring it back to life. Your amygdala (your threat center) is overloaded and sends out stress signals time and time again, and you feel even worse.

When we become aware of our emotional memories, thoughts, and patterns, we can allow the body to experience the feelings, calm the body, and allow everything to land in the present. When the body lands, it can let go of the past, and the old energy is released. Every time we do this, we train the body to let go of old feelings. We hack the old programming and lower the volume of the feelings, breaking their dependency. That's how we reach FREEDOM.

MOLECULES AND MESSAGES

According to leading neuroscientists, such as Candace Pert and Joe Dispenza, each thought, emotion, and feeling creates a molecule, called neuropeptide. These molecules carry emotional messages and affect the chemistry of every cell in our body as they travel through our bloodstreams. When we experience emotions—such as fear, worry, anger, sadness, guilt, excitement, or joy—each separate emotion releases its own mix of neuropeptides. Each cell has thousands of receptors, and each receptor is specific for a peptide. These peptides flow through the body and attach to the matching receptors in the cells, which changes the structure of each cell. When the body responds to a thought with a feeling, the brain releases chemicals into a loop, so thoughts create feelings and feelings create thoughts. Our hormone system simply receives chemical messages through molecules that make us feel what we are thinking. This loop of repeated chemicals causes the cells in the body to react. For example, if we have a happy thought, our system is filled with neuropeptides that can have an uplifting effect. However, if we have repetitive negative thought patterns, our cells may not function properly, which can lead to us feeling bad.

Something interesting happens when the cells divide. If a cell has been exposed to a particular peptide more than another, the new cell produced by the divide will have more of the receptors that match the specific peptide. In addition, the new cell has fewer receptors for peptides the parent cell is not exposed to as often. If we bombard our cells with peptides from negative thoughts, we program our cells to accept more negative peptides in the future. What's even worse is we reduce the number of receptors for positive peptides in the cells, which can give us a negative outlook.

There are always discussions about which one comes first, the thought or the feeling. Instead, imagine a stream of information moving through your nervous system, a mass of electrical signals that rush back and forth, most of which occur unconsciously. Every time you think a thought, a biochemical reaction occurs in your brain. Chemical signal substances are released and sent to the body, which begin to feel what you are thinking. As you begin to feel what you think, the brain notes that the body feels a certain way and creates more thoughts that correspond to the sensation in the body. And this is how it goes, back and forth, back and forth. The more thoughts you have, the more chemical signal substances are produced, and then more feelings that reflect your thoughts are created. In the end, you have created a state of mind.

When you realize that your thoughts and feelings can affect your body's response and also its health, and the body, in turn, can affect your thoughts and feelings, you understand how important it is to change your thought patterns, as you learned to do in Chapter 3.

HUMANS ARE CREATURES OF HABIT

When we have lived with our feelings for a long time, they become a habit. Without them, life feels empty. Even if the feelings are negative, we might choose to hold onto them because it feels strange without them. Neuroscientist Joe Dispenza highlights a good example of guilt. If you often think, "It's my fault," your body starts to produce guilt chemicals, and after a while, your cells are swimming in a sea of guilt. The receptors in the cells are becoming more and more susceptible to these chemicals, and suddenly, it feels normal to constantly feel a sense of guilt. That which is normal for the body eventually starts to feel good. Much like sitting in a loud office: In the end, you have become so used to all of the sounds that you no longer hear them.

After a while, your cells become insensitive and your body needs to feel more guilt to feel alive. You have become addicted to guilt and feeling guilty becomes your normal state of mind. Your body needs to experience stronger emotions because it has a chemical addiction. When your cells don't get their dose of guilt, they start to worry. The brain has taught the body that it should receive a certain dose. You have changed your receptors and your biochemistry, so feeling guilt has become the correct chemical balance. If you change the balance, the cells protest because they feel weird and uncomfortable. Because we are habitual, we want what is familiar, what we recognize. It's not always what's good for us, just what's familiar. When we try to break the patterns, the body says, "I don't like this. I feel insecure. I don't recognize myself." The body tries to stop us. This explains why we sometimes cling to our feelings and sometimes even search for and hold on to the negative feelings we are familiar with.

THIS IS HOW I AM

Feelings are the end product of an experience. We will react when something happens in our lives. The important thing is how *long* we react. If we let the emotional reaction last for a long time, it eventually becomes part of our identity. That's when we define ourselves with the feeling and claim, "This is how I am." We remain in our emotions, in the chemical remnants of the past.

Once the feelings have become part of our identity, it is very difficult to let go. Letting go of a feeling is letting go of a part of ourselves, which creates fears in most of us. We invest a lot in creating our identity. Therefore, we often want to hold onto our feelings so we know who we are. When I work with clients, I often hear, "If I let go of the problem/feeling/thought/behavior, who do I become?" For many, it is a scary thought to not know who you are. This means that we unconsciously look for something, an event or a person, to recreate the feeling, since it has become our identity. We repeat feelings over and over again, to confirm who we think we are. A lot of people are afraid of personal development or change because it means we leave behind the reality and security we have created. We can become just as dependent on our old feelings and our own identity as we can become addicted to alcohol, coffee, cigarettes, or chocolate. The body wants us to return to the familiar feeling and a familiar state of mind.

CLIENT STORY

What Was I Supposed to Do?

Sophie was constantly worried about her studies, her future, not living up to expectations, failing, and even succeeding. The first seed of anxiety was sown when Sophie's grandmother died; Sophie was only three years old. Sophie was very close to her grandmother and felt powerless when she disappeared. The little girl didn't understand what was happening, she had no answers, and she turned to the adults around her in the hope they would have answers. Her belief was that she had no answers, so she had to turn to others for answers and advice. Others seemed to know more. Not having the answers herself created a strong anxiety in Sophie. How could she cope with life, when she had no answers, when she didn't know what needed to be done? When Sophie realized that she carried the little three-year-old's confusion into adulthood, she realized that she could let go of the anxiety. In adulthood, she had more resources at her disposal. All she had to do was start listening to herself and give herself some time to hear her own answers.

After a month, Sophie came back and angrily announced to me that she was anxious again, at the same magnitude as before. We continued to work and discovered some more blocks, which we resolved.

Another month later, she came back—hysterical. Nothing had worked. "All my anxiety is back," she said. We started our session but couldn't find anything specific that would explain why the anxiety remained.

After some time of pondering, I asked her subconscious why the anxiety returned. After a moment's silence, the answer came: "But if I let go, what am I supposed to do? Who am I supposed to be?" The anxiety had become such a strong part of her personality that without it, she didn't know who she would be or what she would do. The fear of not knowing who she was without her anxiety made her cling to it and bring it back.

In such cases, you have to really highlight the benefits of changing one's personality. Today, Sophie's anxiety is completely gone, and she is enjoying her new personality—a confident, forward, and happy woman.

FEELINGS CAN BE UNPLEASANT

Diving deep into your emotional life can be scary for many because it is usually not the most exciting feelings that we encounter at first. We will meet what we have pushed aside. There can also be a fear of letting out our feelings—that we will not be able to handle them or will drown in them. But if we don't let them out, we end up so full of feelings that we almost drown in them anyway.

There are two important principles about feelings:

1. When we allow ourselves to fully express the emotional experience, the cycle ends, and the feeling leaves us when it has done its thing.
2. If we fight against the emotional experience, it will continue to be repeated and maybe even get stronger each time. The body is trying to communicate something, and if you don't listen, the body will do what it needs to deliver its message.

When we are children, we cannot handle strong feelings or conflicts ourselves. As adults, our subconscious mind remembers how hard and uncomfortable some of our feelings felt when we were children, and we prefer not to experience them again. The fear that we won't be able to handle our feelings, even though we are adults, can remain in the subconscious, and we then choose different strategies to distract or numb the uncomfortable feelings.

- We might stay in our heads. I usually call it moving up to the attic. We analyze, compare, criticize, consider, discuss, control, and try to think away the feeling.
- We distract ourselves in various ways, such as with work, shopping, alcohol, cigarettes, exercise, sex, food, gambling, or simply being too busy. We get distracted by new, exciting things and lose focus on what is important, the so-called Shiny Object Syndrome (SOS).
- We talk about our experiences and feelings endlessly instead of actually feeling them. We take in the opinions of others and describe everything we experience in detail.
- We push the emotion aside, ignore it, or push it down.

- We shut down and feel nothing at all. We simply check out.
- We create an artificial self, a mask we show instead.

Most of us distract and numb painful feelings every now and then. The question is whether it is a good idea. Every time we distract or numb our feelings, it comes with a price tag. The question is, is it worth the cost?

CAN WE CONTROL OUR FEELINGS?

You probably recognize the experience of knowing logically how you should or shouldn't react. You know you don't have to be afraid of certain things or react like you do in certain situations. Still, you can't resist when the feeling takes over.

With a little training, you can control what you think about the feeling, how you interpret it, and how you act. Knowledge is the first step, but it is not enough. We can know what steps we need to take or why the problem exists, but more information doesn't always make it easier for us to change the behavior. We know more, but nothing happens. Our conscious, logical mind wants to have a lot of information and know all the steps to take, preferably in what order, too. The subconscious that is governed by emotions and programming doesn't work that way. Do you remember the elephant? The subconscious mind is the elephant, and you are the conscious mind riding on the top. You can fight to steer in one direction, but if the elephant wants to go in another direction, it will be difficult to steer the right way. The solution is to get to know the elephant and understand why it is pulling in the opposite direction.

YODA MOMENT

Negative feelings are a signal that something wants your attention, just like physical pain. A panic attack is a "wake up call," something is trying to get your attention. The symptoms are messengers trying to tell you something is wrong. The body can't tell you in words, so through different signals, it tries to explain what is wrong. If you deactivate the signal with alcohol, food, work, exercise, medicine, or shopping, it will never be heard. You need to understand why the signal is there. You may find that a small five-year-old child within you is controlling your life, even though you are an adult.

- What signals are your body sending you? What do you think they mean?
- What do you long for?
- What do you need?
- What has happened in your life lately?
- Do you feel pain anywhere or is your body tense?
- What feelings remain in you?
- When was the last time you talked openly about your feelings?
- If you see yourself from the outside, what do you see?
- What strategies do you use to distract yourself from and to numb unwanted feelings?

JEDI MIND TRICKS

When feelings come up to the surface, you can't ignore them. Pushing down or fighting them doesn't work; neither does burying them with affirmations or distracting yourself in different ways. Instead, you need to understand that the emotions are there for a reason and that you are the one who created them. Don't spend time trying to change people, situations, or experiences. Dive into your emotional life and look at what beliefs and feelings are beneath the surface. Most feelings disappear quickly when fully experienced. When we fight the feelings, they get stuck inside us.

HACK #11

BECOME FRIENDS WITH THE FEELINGS

No one can guarantee we will never get angry, sad, disappointed, or feel any other unwanted feelings. But we can decide that our feelings shouldn't hurt anyone—others or ourselves. By working with yourself and your programming, you can become aware of negative feelings before you respond to them. You can take control and express them in the best possible way.

Awareness is the first important key to becoming friends with one's feelings. When a feeling arises, let it come out. Experience the feeling in the body. Make note of everything you experience. Describe the sensation. How do you experience the feeling? Is it weight, a material, or an object? Does it have any color, shape, or temperature? Where in the body is it? Does it move? From where does the feeling come? Can you recognize it from earlier in your life? What happened? Do you need to experience the feeling the same way today as an adult? How can you change it?

If you don't want to wait for a moment when a feeling emerges, you can sit down, close your eyes, and do this as an exercise. Reflect and write down what you feel in your journal. Another way to get to know your feelings is to share them with someone you trust or go to a therapist or coach.

Being friends with your feelings means they won't scare you as much. Think of feelings like messengers, just like the oil indicator in a car, conveying messages, things you need to look at.

⊶ HACK #12

HIT THE PAUSE BUTTON

Few people have learned to deal with their emotions. We are told we should calm down, control ourselves, relax, or just stop it. Rarely, we are told how to actually do these things. Everything that happens inside us is biochemistry, even feelings. Sometimes, it may be enough to be five minutes late or spill our coffee to upset our feelings and, thus, our biochemistry. Did you know that an emotional state only lasts for ninety seconds?

When something happens that affects us, a ninety-second process starts in the body. The stress hormone cortisol pumps into our systems, the feelings flood us, and our bodies fall into a state of readiness. The exciting thing is that after these *ninety seconds,* we have a choice whether we stay in the emotional loop or not. We can either continue the cycle or shift our focus to a more positive thought process. You can observe and experience the process and then witness how it disappears. It's fascinating. If, after ninety seconds, you continue to feel anger, fear, disappointment, or worry, you need to consider which thoughts stimulate the parts in the brain that create the reaction over and over again. Of course, the ninety-second process doesn't apply if you are processing a deeper sadness or have experienced trauma.

The body warns you before the wave of feelings occur. How does your body react? Are you getting red? Does your heart beat faster? Do your hands start trembling? Do you feel a knot in your stomach? Are you restless? Studies show that your body can experience feelings long before your brain understands what is happening. Therefore, it is important to notice the changes in your body before the feelings take over. How do you experience the feeling that is on the rise? For me, it's a flutter just below the sternum. I get restless and want to move.

Now, you have to hit the pause button, take control of the feelings, and calm down the body for the first ninety seconds. The most effective way is to activate the vagus nerve, the longest nerve in the body, which actually consists of two separate nerve pathways that run from the brain stem to the intestine and which connects the brain with all of the important organs in the body. The vagus nerve turns off the "fight-or-flight" function and helps you regain control. You can activate the vagus nerve by moving, breathing deeply and slowly, getting a massage, meditating, or taking a cold shower.

Here are some #mindhacks that you can try during the ninety seconds that the cortisol is rushing around in your body.

- Breathe deeply and slowly. Inhale and count to five; exhale and count to five. When we breathe, we create a space for the process. We can more easily reach and understand our feelings, allowing them to ebb out before creating a response.
- Be aware of what you are feeling, but do not give in to the feelings. Count to ninety and remind yourself you have a choice.
- Move. Get up from the chair. Take a walk
- Rinse your face, neck, or throat with cold water.
- Visualize. What results do you want to achieve, and how do you want to feel? Engage the entire brain by activating all of your senses. What do you see, hear, feel, smell, and taste?

Try to find what works for you. What can you do in the first ninety seconds to manage your stress response? Do you recognize this stress reaction from your childhood? Do you need to be equally stressed today as back then?

The important thing is that you control the process until the explosion because, once you explode, it is difficult to control the feelings. Use the pause button, take a deep breath, and let the feelings do their thing for ninety seconds.

After each thought comes a new thought . . . and another and another. If you choose to think positive thoughts after calming down your body, it actually takes less than forty-five seconds to redirect the thought to something positive, if you do it actively. Change the direction of your mind for forty-five seconds, and you will be able to change both your feelings and behavior. Feel free to use the startup ritual 5-4-3-2-1-GO as you learned in Chapter 4.

O⟋ HACK #13

THE FIVE-MINUTE TRICK

Sometimes, we need more than ninety seconds to calm down and process our feelings. When something goes wrong and does not turn out as you intended, allow yourself to fully experience all of your feeling for five minutes. Complain, scream, cry, and vent—whatever you need to do to let the feelings pass through your body. When five minutes have passed, you say, "I can't change it." What has happened has happened. It is the resistance to reality, as it is, that causes the pain.

I like the parable of the philosopher Eckhart Tolle. Your car gets a flat tire on a dark forest road, far out in the countryside. You get angry, curse the higher powers, think life is unfair, and kick the tire. Instead, if you accept the reality that you are standing there with a flat tire and that nothing can change what has happened, then you can start looking ahead. Acceptance doesn't mean sitting down and giving up or accepting unfair situations. It's to see the reality as it is and instead focus on opportunities and solutions. But it is okay to first experience the emotional storm.

In the beginning, you will probably think five minutes feels inadequate, that you need much more than five minutes to get all your emotions out. But when five minutes have passed, focus on something other than what has happened. Start focusing on solutions. Gradually, you will be able to keep your unwanted feelings within your allotted five minutes and eventually, you may only need a short period to vent. You have begun to accept the reality as it is.

⊶ HACK #14

CHANGE THE LABEL

During an experience, our brains collect information about what is happening in our bodies, interpret the physical sensations, and put an emotional label on everything. The label can be called worry, fear, joy, security, and so on.

What many people don't realize is that some feelings are experienced the same way in the body, but we put different labels on them. Imagine you're in line to ride the roller coaster at an amusement park. Your heart beats faster, you feel aroused, the cortisol levels increase, and your body prepares for action. Would you put the labels of worry, nervousness, or fear on the physical sensations you are experiencing? Or would you use the labels excited, expectant, playful, or fired up? Maybe you would even use the label frightened delight—both fear and exaltation at the same time.

When you are anxious (or nervous) and exalted (or expectant, excited, or fired up), the same sensations are produced in the body. The same things happen physiologically. The only difference is the label you put on the feeling. What would happen if you changed the label? When you are worried or nervous, think, "I am excited, expectant, excited, fired up." When you say positive things to yourself, you prevent the cortisol from getting into your brain and taking over. When you redefine your anxiety and nervousness into a positive state, your prefrontal cortex, the executive boss, works better. When your brain is not filled with cortisol, it becomes easier to think clearly, make good decisions, and move forward.

CHAPTER 5 IN 60 SECONDS

- Feelings are energy in motion. Feelings that are avoided or suppressed take energy from you.
- Stored feelings are like chemical archives and can be activated by your thoughts.
- Negative feelings are messengers trying to say that something is wrong.
- Suppressed emotions often explode elsewhere.
- **Become friends with the emotions.** Examine the feelings. When you understand them, they become less scary.
- **Hit the pause button.** After ninety seconds of emotional storm, you can choose whether or not to stay in the emotional loop.
- **The Five-Minute Trick.** When something goes wrong, allow yourself to fully experience all your feelings for five minutes. After five minutes, start looking ahead. What can be done?
- **Change the label.** Replace a negative label with something reinforcing and positive, such as an anchor thought.

CHAPTER 6

CONQUER THE FEAR

*Fears are shrinking your brain capacity. You make worse decisions, your
creativity decreases, and you see fewer opportunities and solutions.*

One of our most common and most inhibitory feelings is fear, including
all its variants: anxiety, nervousness, angst, insecurity, helplessness, powerlessness, and the feeling of being overwhelmed. We can be afraid of all
sorts of things: failure, the unknown, not being able to perform, not being liked,
being abandoned, not finding our purpose, and even talking to other people.

How fear silences us in life is different from person to person. How does fear hold
you back? Have you made your world small? Does your fear stop you from trying
new things? Are you thinking too much? Are you avoiding situations or people?

Fears have a number of characteristics:

- Fear spreads like a weed. Initially, we may only have a few fears. Gradually, the number increases and, in the end, we are afraid of many
  different things.
- Fear grows over time. When the cortisol is flooding the brain, it has a tendency to magnify the problem and what we fear becomes insurmountable.

- Fear shuts down the rational, analytical part of the brain. We make hasty decisions that can cause problems.

- Fear shrinks our brains and stifles our creativity. We see fewer opportunities and solutions.

- Fear can be triggered by a variety of things. You may remember the horse rider, Cecilia, whose fear was triggered when she passed the riding hall door. The door reminded her of an unstable home growing up. Our fears can be triggered many things: an object, a time of day, a sound, a person, a scent, or a scene in a TV show or movie.

- Some fears may have their cause in something completely different. The brain doesn't like abstract fears, such as the fear of what others think of you, the fear of not being able to handle things, or the fear of the unknown. My experience is that the brain seems to change the fear into something more concrete and visible—for example aircrafts, heights, or water—because those threats are tangible and can both be seen and avoided. Therefore, the brain thinks the problem is solved. A fear can also be a misinterpretation in the brain. When we first become afraid of something, the brain takes a snapshot of its surroundings and interprets it. The fear is real, but the cause of the fear is a misinterpretation.

CLIENT STORY

I Can't Find My Way

Sara was afraid of water and of getting under the water. She needed to feel her feet on the sea floor, be close to the edge of the pool, or swim with someone to feel safe.

During our session, Sara sensed a strong confusion. "I can't find my way," she said. As a five- or six-year-old, Sara was already driven and goal-oriented, unlike her parents who were happy with their places in life. The little girl needed help clarifying her goals and finding tools to achieve them. When she didn't get this, she lost her footing and the direction she would take in life. How do you find your way forward when you are only five or six years old, and no one is there to show you? When Sara swam and lost contact with the sea floor or dove under the water, the feeling of not being able to orientate, not finding her own foundation to stand on, was triggered. So it wasn't the water that Sarah was afraid of. The water triggered the deeper fear.

After her session, Sara was able to bathe, swim, and dive completely without any problems. In addition, she found her own foundation to stand on and her own path in her career.

 Take a moment and consider if any of your fears might be about something else.

ANXIETY AND PANIC ATTACKS

Anxiety and panic attacks are expressions of fear. Many who seek my help with anxiety and panic attacks claim the problem arose quite suddenly in their lives, but when we take a closer look, that often turns out to be false. Anxiety and panic attacks don't come suddenly. They start quite often when we are not taking care of ourselves for a long time.

We compromise and satisfy everyone else before ourselves. We become tired and stressed . . . then unbalanced. We start to worry about the future and not being able to cope. We feel frustrated and annoyed and start having difficulty sleeping. Perhaps, to keep our energy levels up, we drink more coffee. Our brains are now set on high beta waves, and the survival mechanism kicks in, which you will learn more about in Chapter 8.

You are not feeling well, but you are pushing through your day because that is just the way it is. Suddenly, one day when you are on your way home from work and are stuck between everyone on the bus, you start feeling strange. Your breathing increases, your heart beats harder, and your field of vision decreases. You are having a panic attack. Your brain is now taking pictures of the surroundings to determine what it is that is making you scared and stressed. "Aha," the brain says, "it's crowds (or possibly buses)."

As I mentioned in Chapter 2, the brain takes snapshots of the environment when something happens and then links these images to danger. The information is stored in the subconscious, which then works actively to avoid these dangerous situations. Unfortunately, the brain has made a mistake in its analysis. It is not crowds or buses that are the cause of the panic attack, it is all the stress you have been experiencing lately, maybe even for years. All the stress, worry, and irritation you have been pushing down for a long time has created a ticking bomb that just happened to explode on the bus.

Now, the snowball effect begins. You start to worry about the panic attacks because you don't know when they will come. The body can have a panic attack without your consent. You can't ride the bus; you can't meet people, and you can't travel. Your world is shrinking. You start eating medication for anxiety, but you still avoid buses or crowds. You start therapy and try to figure out the fear, which sometimes works, but the discomfort still persists, even if you can now control your emotions a little better. You start smoking, drinking, or eating to unwind, but the anxiety remains. You get scared of more things because the fear is spreading like a weed.

The solution is to look at what has been stressing you. Thoughts, feelings, habits, and behaviors. You need to slow down and observe yourself, which you will learn more about in Chapter 8. In the beginning, it can be difficult to slow down because the body doesn't want to face the emotions. You may feel restless or irritated or that it's completely impossible for you to unwind. But with discipline and a willingness to meet the emotions and solve the problem, the body will eventually trust that you can handle what you face.

FEAR OF LOSING CONTROL

When I work with my clients, we often come down to the same root cause when it comes to fear: a lack of control. When we have no control or if there is a risk that we may lose control, we become afraid. It is a natural human desire to strive for control because it makes us feel safe and secure. We know where we are going and what we can expect. There are two types of control: internal and external. Studies show that if we have a sense of inner control, that is, we can influence a result, control ourselves, control our emotions, and control our lives, we feel happier.

If we don't have this internal control, we often try to control something outside ourselves, including people, possessions, and situations. We try to control what we can. If you can have control over yourself, your feelings, your results, and your life, you create a sense of security, safety, and POWER.

The disadvantage of wanting to have control over everything is that we may avoid people and situations that make us insecure, nervous, or afraid. If we silence ourselves or run away from challenges, opportunities, and others, we will never have a sense of control. Fear wins and we have lost. To feel genuine control, we need to face our fears.

The fear of losing control often stems from when we were children. We became afraid of experiences in our surroundings that we couldn't control. We couldn't control our father's mood. We couldn't prevent our parents from divorcing. We couldn't influence which team picked us in gym class. Losing control is scary; and therefore, children find a way to deal with it. What strategies did you create as a child to avoid feeling scared and which of these have you taken with you into adulthood? Do you become silent? Do you turn the situation into a joke? Do you flee the situation? Are you trying to be perfect? Each time you are exposed to an old fear, your old matrix, which was installed as a child, is activated, and you react without thinking. It is important to understand that we don't need to have experienced what we define as major trauma to be afraid of losing control or feeling unsuccessful. As a child, moments of uncertainty or inability to perform can feel like a very big thing.

CLIENT STORY

No, No, No . . .

Renata felt uncertain about her abilities and didn't dare to be herself. As a child, Renata was shy, but otherwise, her childhood was "very good," as she herself put it. We examined the feeling of not fully being herself and trusting her own abilities. Renata immediately picked up on a memory where she, as a two-year-old, sat and played on the floor with her toys. She played without much enthusiasm. She was bored. Renata decided to do something different and walked out to the kitchen. The sun was shining through the window, and Renata became so fascinated that she climbed up on a chair, and then the table, to explore. When Renata's mother discovered her daughter on the kitchen table, she came running, shouting, "No, no, no . . ." and immediately took her down from the table—a perfectly normal reaction from a mother. After all, something dangerous could have happened. But what was Renata's interpretation?

Renata remembered how her mother often said, "No, no, no" and "stop, be careful, beware, wait" when Renata, as a little girl, wanted to explore the world. After a while, the little girl began to explore less and less. Renata realized she had created a rule for herself: She must have the approval from an adult authority to take initiative and do new things. She couldn't trust her own ability to assess situations and how to deal with them. In adulthood, Renata was still seeking approval from someone else who seemed to know more than herself before acting.

THE ALARM GOES OFF

When you encounter something you are afraid of or are doing something unpleasant, an alarm goes off in the body, and the body responds long before you understand what is happening. How does your body react? How do you experience the fear? Does your face become red? Do you feel warm or cold? Do you feel nausea? Does your heart beat faster? Do your hands start trembling? Do you feel a knot in your stomach? Are you feeling restless?

The sensations in the body are warnings that something dangerous could happen, and it is best to sit back and lie low. The body tries to slow you down to prevent you from doing something dangerous. If your dad got angry when you were too loud when he came home from work, you may be worried and feel a knot in your stomach as soon as you hear your boss come in through the door at work. Or if your classmates giggled when you were speaking in front of the class at school, your cheeks may heat up every time you give a presentation at work. Your body remembers the times people and situations were perceived as dangerous and the information is stored for future use. When you, as an adult, meet people and situations that are reminiscent of experiences where you had no control or where you failed, were scared, or got hurt, you might react exactly as you did when you were a child. Your brain shouts, "Danger! Lie low; Don't do it!"

THE AUTOPILOT IS ACTIVATED

When the alarm goes off and the body responds, the autopilot is activated. You automatically select the strategies you have used throughout your life. Maybe you start to hesitate and find all sorts of ways to postpone what you need to do. Or you worry so much about what to say to a certain group and how they would perceive you, that you don't say anything at all. Or you imagine everything that can go wrong, and you analyze every detail and how to do the right thing. Your subconscious interprets what happens in your adult life the same way you did when you were a child. You usually choose the same strategies to face the fear as when you were a child. And although strategies, such as avoiding, fleeing, hesitating, overthinking the situation, or becoming quiet, angry, or indifferent can give you a sense of control for the moment, they give you no real control over your life. The fear follows you everywhere, and you will have a hard time creating the opportunities you want.

THE FEAR SILENCES YOU

What patterns do you repeat from childhood? The more you notice these patterns, the easier it is to master them. Here are some common strategies—so-called excuses—that we use to try to master the fears:

I Have to Think About It

To think is not to act. Thinking gives you the sense you are working on the problem, but in reality, you are not really doing anything. You are living inside your head and bouncing back and forth in your brain channels, paralyzing yourself with a million different outcomes or strategies. When you overthink, you are drained of energy and, ultimately, have no power left to act. In the event of a change, you will feel fear, for you are embarking on new and unknown territory. The instinct to silence the fear makes you stop and think. What should I do? How can I get it right? What if it doesn't work? What happens if I choose this? Overthinking is a way to stay safe inside your head, much like a sprinter that gets stuck in the starting blocks. You never have to risk anything or face the fear of not succeeding. It just feels safer to think about the problem than to act on it. This gives you a false sense of control.

I Can't Do It

There are many reasons why the notion of "I can't do it" has taken hold. An anxious parent can unknowingly slow down a child's development, as in the example of Renata. Many adults have retained the belief since childhood that they *can't* do something. There are no opportunities or solutions to their problems. It is called learned helplessness, and it is the children in them who were once helpless, who still feels this way. Being tough on ourselves is another variant of "I can't." We judge ourselves and our efforts. Being over-critical can also be a way of gaining control over the fear of being criticized. If we are hard on ourselves, we gain control over our own pain. We hurt ourselves before anyone else has the chance. If anyone else criticizes us, we have already done it ourselves, so the pain is less.

Saying, "I can't" can also be a strategy to avoid doing what we are afraid of. Just as in the previous example with Elsa, the one who discovered that when she was scared, she could just say, "I can't do it," and everyone came to her rescue. Quite often, she didn't have to do what she was afraid of. In the moment, it may feel good to avoid the situation, but then we will never experience the joy—and pride—in being able to handle things by ourselves.

This Is How It Is

We already know if it will work or not. We have tried before or we just know. The know-it-all in us closes the door for new opportunities because we already know and understand everything.

Everything Is Fine

We don't dare to see the truth, so we say that everything is fine. "It's not that dangerous. It's fine as it is. I'm okay. It's working fine." We do everything to preserve our illusion because we dare not see reality as it is. The fear that we will not be able to cope with the consequences or that there is no solution to the problem leads to us accepting people and situations that are not good for us.

I Don't Care

Many hide their fear behind a mask of indifference. We play it cool and act uninterested. The fear that something will go wrong and that we will be judged is so great that we focus on finding all the flaws and why it cannot be done.

It Has to Be Perfect

Another way to avoid fear and gain control is to plan everything in advance and then make everything perfect. Being perfect is a way to avoid criticism. The problem with perfectionism is that it paralyzes us and makes us exhausted. The fear of not being good enough, not being perfect, makes us so busy preparing ourselves to do everything perfectly right from the start, that we never get started at all. The perfect opportunity never comes. Once we get started, we micro-manage every step and make both ourselves and our environment go crazy.

It Has to Look Good

This is the little sister of the perfectionist. We must always be perceived as good and proper. Our value is entirely tied to our ability to impress others, so we do nothing that makes us look stupid or that might ruin our image. We worry about what others think and work hard for others to feel good about us and like us, even if it comes at the expense of our own needs.

I'm Afraid of Being Wrong

The fear of making mistakes often comes from the fact we are afraid of being punished, rejected, judged, or ridiculed. The strategy here is to be quiet and invisible or a people-pleaser. If I don't attract attention, people may not see me and, therefore, cannot criticize me. If I make everyone happy, I will be accepted. This is a typical chameleon-type behavior where we adapt to our surroundings. Chameleons are good at reading their environments and understanding what they must do to preserve the peace in any given situation.

CLIENT STORY

The Chameleon

Ronny sought help because he always adapted to others and rarely dared to make his voice heard. It was important to him what others thought of him and that he was acting "right." During our session, Ronny picked up on a memory of how, as a five-year-old, he started the vacuum cleaner to help with the cleaning, which triggered his father's aggression. "The vacuum cleaner was no toy, and the furniture and floors could be damaged," his father said. Ronny recalled that his dad often got angry with him when he did something wrong. Since Ronny, as a child, couldn't predict when the outbreaks would come, it was best to be quiet and cautious. Don't make a fuss and read the surroundings—and especially his father—to be prepared for what could trigger the outbreaks. Ronny became an expert at reading his surroundings and trying to figure out how to act appropriately in all situations. He stopped taking initiative and became a skilled chameleon.

The programming to become invisible and adapt to avoid criticism remained in Ronny even as an adult. For Ronny, it was about making his voice heard, without the fear that the surroundings would explode like his father had.

When we don't say or do things out of fear of being wrong, we silence ourselves. Over time, more and more events are stacked on top of one another, and in the end, everything we pushed down can resurface as anger, panic, anxiety, rashes, and headaches, among other things.

Here it is important to understand that you may have become a chameleon or a people-pleaser to survive. In these cases, it is not a personality trait or desire to be loved but a survival instinct, a security measure to create peace in your surroundings so that no one can harm you. If so, it is a good idea to seek professional help.

I'm Afraid of Failure

The fear of failure often comes from black-and-white, all-or-nothing thinking. Either I'm smart or stupid, good or bad, brave or cowardly. Psychologist Carol Dweck calls this a fixed mindset. This means our understanding of our abilities is that they're fixed; we simply have certain qualities and skills, or we don't. We must constantly prove we are smart or talented. A failure is the same as a setback and means we are not smart or have any talent. For example, if we get a bad result on a test, we are no longer smart. We may think we are pretty good at something, but then there will be a moment when we fail and instantly crash. When we have a fixed mindset, we don't believe we can change, evolve, or become better at something. *This is just how I am . . .*

For many years, I thought I was bad at sports. My classmates confirmed this by often choosing me last when it came to ball games. My sports teacher told me I needed to try harder. In the end, I still couldn't catch a ball if my life depended on it.

On a holiday trip a number of years ago, the hotel offered tennis lessons. I decided to examine if I really was that bad at sports. After an hour of playing, the tennis instructor told me I was pretty good; I just needed more training. I started playing tennis, and my self-confidence returned. Today, I hit the ball more times than I miss it.

When we have a fixed mindset, we strive for safe results we believe are within our reach. If things become too challenging, and we don't feel smart or talented, we lose interest. We believe success is about being more talented than others; that failures determine who we are, and that effort is for those who cannot achieve results based on pure talent. If we are smart and talented, we should not have to work for it. We are afraid to feel stupid or like a failure, so we stop challenging ourselves. We believe that if we are smart, we don't make mistakes. We want to be sure to succeed. Smart people should always succeed. Therefore, many with this mindset give up too quickly. They think they lack talent or that it is too difficult for them—in essence, that they are not able.

Instead of being controlled by fear, we should switch to a growth mindset, which is about challenging oneself to learning new things and grow. With a growth mindset, we understand that it is the effort that makes us smart and talented. We understand we have to work for what we want, and sometimes, we have to work really hard. When we are unsuccessful, it may be because we didn't work hard enough and not because we are stupid or untalented. When we succeed in something, it is because we made every effort and earned it. It is about how much work and commitment we put in. We see and praise our efforts because we understand it is the effort that counts.

Boxer Muhammad Ali is an interesting example of a "non-talent," one with a growth mindset, and thanks to this, he became the world champion of boxing. Boxing experts over the years have required certain physical dimensions to identify a natural boxing talent: the dimensions of the knuckles, the boxer's reach, his breast measurement, and his weight. Muhammad Ali didn't have the right dimensions. He was fast, but he didn't have the physics of a really big boxer. He didn't have the strength or the classic moves, and his technique was completely wrong. Sonny Liston, Ali's opponent, was a natural talent. He had everything—the size, strength, and experience. On paper, it was impossible for Ali to win a match against Liston, but Ali's strength was his mindset. Ali carefully studied not only Liston's boxing style, but also the type of person he was. Ali read everything he could about Liston, talked to the people who knew him, and tried to create a picture of how Liston thought and worked. He then used this against Liston. Ali showed off a crazy side before the fight. He knew that if he could make Liston think he was capable of anything, then Liston would see nothing but his big mouth attitude, and that was all Ali wanted him to see. Then came the knockout. Ali's dedication to learning and developing made him a winner. Devotion trumps talent.

So give yourself praise and encouragement that focuses on the effort you put into meeting the challenge, such as endurance, determination, and flexibility. And before you are disappointed with yourself because you may have a fixed mindset, it's good to know that it is perfectly normal to switch between a fixed and a growth mindset in different situations and in different areas. We are never either completely fixed or dynamic in our approach.

I'm Just Going To . . .

We prepare to feel safe. We postpone things in the belief that the longer we wait, the safer we become. Meanwhile, we find a million other things to do. The problem is the longer we wait, the more uncertain we become. It will never be the right time. It is also easy to become overwhelmed when facing a major project. There is so much to be done, so much uncertainty. We get scared. Then it becomes easier to distract ourselves with something less important. Replying to a few emails, making a call, emptying the dishwasher, doing errands, or checking Instagram. When we distract ourselves, there is nothing wrong with us; it could be the goal or the project that is too big. We see the obstacles instead of the opportunities. We think, and think, and think. In the end, we can't cope with all thoughts about what needs to be done, and we become paralyzed.

It Is More Convenient . . .

Many of us mask our fears as practicality. It is more convenient to stay in this workplace right now. It is better to wait with furthering my education until next year. It is better to wait until the children get older. The truth is that we are afraid to choose something new. What we really want seems impossible to reach and ridiculous to expect, so we choose the practical.

I Have Too Much Work to Do

Our brain is quite inventive when it comes to hiding from fear and not having to face it. Did you know that being too busy is one way to hide from fear? When we are busy with everything that needs to be done in life, we don't need to change. We don't have time. If we slow down, we start to feel. Slowing down means we have to face ourselves and our fears. We need to see the truth about a situation or learn something about ourselves, either of which may be uncomfortable. We don't dare to stop and face the situation; instead, we rush on with life. The problem is when we are fully occupied with trivial things, such as responding to emails, checking social media, or watching TV, we may feel we aren't really accomplishing anything in life, which can cause feelings of emptiness and dissatisfaction.

In conclusion, there are a variety of strategies we use when we are scared. And they all work on autopilot. But now, it's time to regain control and conquer the fear.

 YODA MOMENT
Take a moment and write in your journal:

- What are you scared of, worried about, or nervous about? Do you feel helpless, powerless, insecure, or overwhelmed?

- What happens in your body when you feel scared?
- How are you held back or silenced by your fears?
- What strategies do you use when you're scared?
- When we are busy, we don't have time to face our fears. What do you avoid by constantly being busy?
- What, in your childhood, made you create the strategies you still use as an adult when you're scared?
- What couldn't you handle in your childhood that made you feel helpless?
- In what ways were you criticized as a child?

⚙ JEDI MIND TRICKS

Meditating, using positive anchor thoughts, collecting gold nuggets, setting goals and having tools to move forward is good, but there will always be moments when you experience fear, nervousness, or worry. You cannot be completely free of fear because it is part of the human experience. Fear will always be a part of your life, but you can decide how big a part it will take up. You need to learn how to face your fears. Taking control of the fear is not just about thinking positive thoughts but also about controlling your mental game. For years, you have reacted to your fears in a specific way—so often that it has become a habit. You no longer reflect on how you react; your autopilot has taken over.

The first step in controlling your fear is to see the moments when you are silent, angry, avoidant, or fleeing. When you use these strategies, know they are there to protect you, trying to help you feel as if you are in control, but in reality, you give up your control. You choose the same strategy you did as a child, which will probably not help you reach your potential, solve your problem, or move forward in life. Strategies that perhaps protected you and gave you a sense of control as a child are, today, strategies that prevent you from getting anything done.

⌐ HACK #15

SLOW DOWN

Fear often makes us think too big. "What should I do with my life?" "How should I solve all my problems?" It becomes overwhelming, and we find it difficult to come up with solutions or see new opportunities. To gain control over the fear, we need to slow down. As we slow down, our prefrontal cortex, the executive boss, starts to work better, and we can break down the problem into smaller parts.

The fear that we will not be able to manage things or get what we want in life can make us stressed and absent-minded. The stress does not allow us to experience things in the moment, but rather, to rush past everything. When we say, "I don't have time" all the time—which I have said countless times—it eventually becomes a fact. The stress, fear, and worry eat up our time, as the brain uses time to worry instead of doing anything concrete. Stress, fear, and worry also burn our energy. Our nervous systems pay dearly for constantly being on the brink of what we're afraid of and worried about.

Slowing down helps you hear your inner dialogue. Do you have a fixed or a growth mindset? What do you say to yourself when you face challenges, try something new, or fail?

That's how I am . . .

I'm so bad at . . .

I can't . . .

I have no talent.

It doesn't work . . .

This dialogue means you have a fixed mindset and need to change your thoughts into a more positive and constructive pattern. A growth mindset means you understand it is your effort that makes you smart and talented. You need to praise your efforts and the work you put in to get where you want. It's all about the work!

You can slow down in many different ways. Some ways to relax are to meditate, be in nature, take a bath, read a book, go for a run, play games, or cook. Choose something that clears your mind. In Chapter 8, you will learn more #mindhacks for slowing down.

⚬━ HACK #16

DARE TO AND YOU WILL WIN

Start by looking for situations where you react in non-constructive ways and slow yourself down. Be kind to yourself, and see that you created this strategy once to protect yourself. Although the strategy sometimes works today, it doesn't help you have a healthy control over your life. Take responsibility for your pattern by changing it. When you are about to overcome your fear and dare to do something that feels uncomfortable or scary, your natural response will be to avoid what you are afraid of. Your physical response is encoded in your nervous system. Your body will be alarmed and encourage you to flee. Your subconscious will warn you that something may go badly if you encounter what you're afraid of. Press the pause button for ninety seconds as you learned in Chapter 5, and wait for the emotional storm to calm down. Or count from 5-4-3-2-1-GO as you learned in Chapter 4 and get started. Remember that you only have five seconds to act before your brain hijacks you. Be prepared for your body to try to stop you with any and all possible symptoms.

The only way to retrain your body's response is to face what you are afraid of. When you see the pattern—when you react, how your body reacts, what strategy you choose—you can change it and regain control. You can't wait for the courage. Facing your fears is something that can be trained, just as with your muscles. We often use the words "I can't." Often, it is actually that we don't want to or dare to. We choose not to face the hard work. What we need to accept is that we will have a lifelong relationship with fear. It will never go away. To win, we still have to dare. When we dare, we feel amazing.

Write a list of things you have stopped yourself from doing because of fear. Choose one thing and do it. You can do it!

O—┰ HACK #17

REPLACE YOUR STRATEGIES

To overcome your fears, you need to replace your old strategies, which you use when you are afraid, with new ones that give you real control. Make a list of the strategies you use today when you are scared and updated strategies you intend to use instead. Below, you will find some general suggestions for how to think about new strategies. Make sure they are practically oriented and include concrete details.

Old Strategy	New Approach
I turn quiet.	I'm going to say my opinion.
I over-think things.	I'm going to do something practical.
I postpone things.	I'm going to start building Legos (see hack #18).
I say "I can't."	I will find out the facts and learn how to . . .
I shop for new things.	I'll throw away, donate, or sell one thing.
I choose the easiest way.	I'll choose what I'm curious about.
I isolate.	I intend to contact a friend.
I act like a clown.	I'm going to show a serious side too.
I get overwhelmed and do nothing.	I'll do something small that takes five minutes

O⚊ HACK #18

BUILD WITH LEGOS

Many people say, "Think big" or "Aim for the stars." My experience is that big goals easily become overwhelming to most, like climbing Mount Everest. Big goals can sometimes paralyze me because I can't see how to get there. I need to shrink my goals and break them down into tiny Lego pieces. This makes the idea of reaching them much easier. The brilliant thing about breaking down the goal into small Lego pieces is that I focus only on building. I have time to think and feel if each Lego piece is in the right place. If not, I'll replace it. After a while I see how something is taking shape. I'm not even certain that what is emerging is what I was thinking from the beginning. My goal transformed into something else, something better. Let me give you an example.

Many years ago, I thought I wanted to work in public relations. I dreamed of getting a job in the PR industry. Once I did, I discovered the job was not at all what I expected, and I didn't like it.

Setting goals can be difficult, as goals are often a mental structure around what we want to achieve. But is the goal really what we want? If we focus on one specific goal, there is a risk of thinking it is precisely the right goal for us. Then we become less flexible. We don't see other opportunities. However, when we break down the goal into small pieces of Legos, we have time to try every piece to see if the big goal suits us. We can more easily adjust and change the direction with each step we take. We learn something about ourselves for each Lego piece we put in place. If one Lego piece feels wrong, we can replace it with another. We become more efficient—saving time and energy—because we don't have to go all the way to the final goal before we discover it may not be where we want to be. We can change direction faster. It may be wonderful to think big, but can control the small steps. Furthermore, it is often the actual exploration that is most exciting. Growing is fun.

To grow doesn't necessarily mean changing jobs, moving, or changing partners. It can be doing something new, which feels fresh and exciting. Think small and change one thing at a time. Start exploring! Some questions that can help you along the way are:

- What small Lego pieces can you add to your life to make it feel new and exciting?
- What Lego piece can you remove to create a better life?
- If you have a goal you know you want to reach, what Lego pieces can you start with? Maybe make a phone call, free up time in your calendar, search for more information, or sign up for a course?
- How do you know you've put a new Lego piece in place? For example, being healthy is not a Lego piece; it is a goal. A Lego piece is something specific, such as joining a workout class. And you will know when it has been placed.
- What is your biggest obstacle to placing new Lego pieces? If the Lego piece is too big, break it down further.
- What can you realistically do every day to get to where you want? Make your first step so small that you can do it every day.
- What do you need to do to remember your daily Lego piece? Alarms on your mobile phone, sticky notes, or notes in your calendar?

Now make a plan for your construction.

O⊸ HACK #19

LIST YOUR FAVORITE EXCUSES

What excuses do you use for not getting started with what needs to be done? Here are some common excuses:

I am too tired.	I have to think about it.	I don't have time.
What if . . .	I can't.	It's not possible.
I have no character.	I have pain in my . . .	It's a bit too far away.
It's not the right time.	I must first . . .	It doesn't matter that much.
I don't know how to do it.	It's boring.	I have no money.

Look at your excuses and be honest.

1. Do you really want to achieve what you say you want to achieve? Does the goal matter to you? Or is the goal not really a priority for you? If so, stop your apologies, change direction, and turn your focus toward something else.

2. If it is a priority for you, but you are scared of the change, or if it's difficult to start the task, pick out a smaller action you can do every day to reach your goal. Choose a small Lego piece that takes a maximum of fifteen minutes or less to accomplish.

O⊸ HACK #20

OWN YOUR SUCCESS

When I coach high-performing individuals, many of them are afraid of the word "satisfied." They believe contentment means to sit down and stop pursuing new goals. Nope! The fear that what you are doing is not enough makes you constantly move on to new goals and wins. You can be satisfied with your current situation, proud of what you have achieved, and at the same time, move forward in life. It is not an either/or scenario. You can be both happy and strive forward. What happens if you replace the word satisfied with fulfilled? For me, it made a difference. Fulfilled sounds more gratifying, I think.

Create an I-did-this list—the opposite of a to-do list. Write down every little achievement you conquered during the day. Or start journaling, and every day, write down what made you feel satisfied or fulfilled in your life that day. What have you achieved that you are proud of? Don't forget the little things, such as getting up on time, doing your morning ritual, or handling the tasks and challenges that arose during the day. Being satisfied creates a feeling of fulfillment, which inspires you to strive for new things to be satisfied with. Being proud is also an antidote to your inner critic and perfectionist tendencies.

Another aspect of never being satisfied is imposter syndrome. Author and civil rights activist Maya Angelou and physicist Albert Einstein both suffered from this. This is the fear that others will find out that we are a scam. When we suffer from imposter syndrome, we don't think we deserve our success. We don't experience our ideas or skills as special, and we will never be satisfied. We think others are as good as we are, we are not special or capable, and, therefore, we don't deserve attention or praise. What we forget is how hard we have worked to become good at what we do. We don't see all the changes we made and everything we have managed. We focus on what we *haven't* done or accomplished. You need to own your changes and see your own efforts. Don't focus on who you were before, and don't judge your mistakes. Look at who you are today. Write down what you have been able to do. What are the signs that you have actually achieved something? Be proud of who you have become.

You can also feel like a scam if you haven't had to put in a lot of effort to reach your goals. I worked with Johan, a young man who thought he was a scam. Johan didn't think he was capable and that he wasn't good enough. The reason for Johan's feeling of being a scam was that his father had arranged for him both a job and an apartment and helped him with extra money. Johan felt he had not created his own successes but had taken shortcuts, so he didn't feel proud of his efforts. If you know you got something for free, cultivate a growth mindset instead; make an effort and invest in something that is important to you. You will be proud of your efforts and no longer feel like a scam.

O—🔑 HACK #21

CULTIVATE A GROWTH MINDSET

You don't need strong self-confidence to have a growth mindset. Even if you don't think you're good at something, you can still devote yourself wholeheartedly to learning more. Here are some good #mindhacks on how to cultivate a growth mindset:

- When something feels challenging, and you're tired or bored and your fixed mindset strikes, don't fall for distractions or the thought of quitting. Take on the challenge.
- Surround yourself with people who challenge you to think in new ways.
- Have you failed at something? What did you learn? How can you use the event to grow?
- Is there something you are not good at but have always wanted to try? Do it.
- See and praise your efforts more than the results. And most importantly, do the work!

CHAPTER 6 IN 60 SECONDS

- Fear shuts down the thinking part of the brain and shrinks your brain capacity. You make bad decisions, reduce your creativity, and see fewer opportunities and solutions.

- When the alarm goes off and the body responds, the autopilot is activated. You often choose the same strategies to face the fear as when you were a child.

- **Slow down.** To gain control over your fear, slow down. Your brain will work better, and you can break down your problem into smaller parts.

- **Dare to and you will win.** Train your body's response by facing what you are afraid of. Choose one thing that you stopped yourself from doing because of fear, and do it!

- **Replace your strategies.** Make a list of the strategies you use today when you are scared and which strategies you intend to use instead.

- **Build with Legos.** Big goals can make you overwhelmed. Break down your goals into tiny Lego pieces. Focus on building and exploring. See where the building is leading you.

- **List your favorite excuses.** The things you don't do . . . are they really a priority for you? Reassess and focus on what is important to you.

- **Own your success.** You can be both happy about where you are today and strive forward at the same time. Write down what you are content with in your life.

- **Cultivate a growth mindset.** Take on the challenges, learn more, and take note of the lessons. See and praise your efforts. And do the work. Devotion trumps talent.

HELLO FRIEND!

To feel like you belong, you push away traits that are not accepted by your surroundings. The separation inside you creates a feeling of loneliness.

L oneliness is not the same as being alone. It has nothing to do with how many people we have around us. We can have family and friends and still feel lonely. Loneliness often feels like an emptiness or sadness that hides deep inside the heart.

How can we feel loneliness even though we're not really alone? There are many reasons. We may feel different or believe no one cares, understands, or meets our needs. We may feel that we are not valuable, loved, or included.

As a child, it is common to sometimes feel lonely or different. We might believe we are the only people in the world who are the way we are. In a way, it's true; we are unique. But we also have many common denominators with other people, such as fears and doubts. I felt alone and different for many years. I felt I rarely fit in anywhere, until I realized that I was an HSP—a highly sensitive person. HSPs read their surroundings, take in more information than others, see more than others might notice, and understand things that others can't. I belong to a minority—around 20 percent of the world's population is an HSP—and I sometimes feel a little different. Today, I highly value my sensitivity because it is what allows me to coach and help transform people's lives as deeply as I do.

Feeling lonely is scary. When we are separated from the group, our survival mechanism is turned on. A child doesn't survive on his or her own; we must belong to a pack. To not belong, be an outcast, or be rejected is as scary as death. Standing alone, for example, in front of a group of people can be perceived as an extremely vulnerable situation. Not being invited also triggers the fear of being left out of the pack.

Belonging gives us a sense of control, which is why it is so important. We often develop a character to hide our problems or insecurities—to fit in. We become the good girl, the clown, the cool one, or the chameleon that adapts to all people and situations. Whatever character we choose to be, it often leads to more loneliness. We hide ourselves and don't give people around us the opportunity to get to know us properly. We begin to feel unseen and alone. Loneliness is, unfortunately, something we can create ourselves.

OUR HUMAN BASIC NEEDS

When our needs are not met, a feeling of loneliness can also arise. *No one sees me, no one cares, and no one loves me.* Many of us don't even know what our needs are because we forget to ask ourselves some basic questions. We have learned to follow others, obey others, and make others happy to be included and praised, but we have often missed what *we* need. Belonging to the herd has become so important that we have lost ourselves—not knowing who we are and what we need. Losing ourselves also creates loneliness. In Chapter 9, you will learn more about finding your internal GPS, which is important for reading your "map."

A first step in creating your own map may be to understand there are a number of basic human needs we all have. It is our job to meet these needs, not simply to trust others to meet them. When we listen and take care of ourselves, we feel independent and strong.

World-renowned coach Tony Robbins says we have six basic human needs that motivate us, even though we are not aware of them. We do everything we can to meet them, either in a good or a less good way, consciously or unconsciously. Some people will give up their goals, dreams, and even values to meet these needs.

Understanding our basic human needs is an easy way to understand ourselves, what choices we make, and what motivates us. We can also use this understanding to learn, predict, and face the behavior of others because when we know what motivates a person, we can more easily understand her or him. Their behavior may not always be positive or effective, but they might not have found a better way to meet their needs. It gives us the capacity to have compassion; we can see it is not about us, and they are not looking to harm us. This allows us to stand more firmly on our needs.

The Six Basic Human Needs Are:
1. Safety/Security
2. Variation
3. Importance
4. Community and Love
5. Growth
6. Contribution and Sharing

Robbins explains the six human basic needs the following way:

Safety/Security
Safety is important from a survival perspective. People with a great need for security don't like change. If something changes, they may become scared, angry, or worried. For them, it is most important to keep everything as it is. You can meet your security needs in a positive way by building internal skills, making wise choices, and surrounding yourself with good people you can trust. Or you can meet the need in a less positive way by never changing your workplace—even though you would like to—staying in a relationship that doesn't work, or rarely trying a new holiday destination.

Variation
The opposite of security is variation. We need variety. It's the spice in life. If you have too little variation in life, you will feel bored. How do you meet your need for variety? You can meet it in a positive way by growing, learning, accepting chal-

lenges, and moving toward new goals. Or you can meet it in a less positive way by never completing projects because you want to move on all the time, being unfaithful, or betting on horses. Some even create their variation in life through food.

Importance

The need to feel important, unique, special, and needed is great in all of us. You can meet the need to feel important by working hard, reaching your goals, acknowledging your own efforts, and helping others. Or you can do it by judging and looking down on others, satisfying others, being a so-called people-pleaser, or buying expensive stuff. Some of us can create the feeling of being important by having "significant problems." From this, we get sympathy and understanding, and we feel important.

Community and Love

One of our deepest fears is that we are not good enough, that we cannot be loved for who we are. You can meet the need for love and community by opening your heart, investing in love, and caring for others. Or you can try to buy love for money, settle for half-bad relationships in order to feel some sort of community, or completely ignore the need for love and community.

Growth

Either we grow or we die. Our relationships grow or die. Our companies are growing or dying. We are created to move forward, grow, and develop. You can meet the need to grow by learning new things, moving toward new goals, and taking on challenges. Or you grow in areas that don't matter to you, or you wait to grow until necessary, such as when you are forced to make a change.

Contribution and Sharing

We enjoy a deep satisfaction when we contribute to something greater than ourselves. Contributing brings joy, both for you and others. You can meet the need to contribute by helping others, donating money to charity, or teaching others your skills. The alternative is to only share when others are watching or when it benefits you.

What Needs Are Most Important to You?

How we rank these six basic needs is different; they can be more or less important to us. Two people may have the same needs but different ways to satisfy them. Most people recognize some or all of the needs, but there are usually some needs that stand out as extra important. The needs we have ranked highest determine the direction in our lives. With me, the need for growth is extra strong. This means that I often make decisions that are, in some way, in line with this need and which absolutely cannot be compromised. If I don't grow, I don't feel satisfied. Which of the six basic needs is most important to you?

When we are clear about our needs, it becomes easier for us to meet them and communicate them to others. The feeling of loneliness diminishes as we come into contact with ourselves and begin to understand what it is we need.

HELLO FRIEND!

What you say to yourself matters most. If you have told yourself enough times that you are alone, it has been transformed into a belief, which your brain lives by. If you suddenly start saying that you have many friends or that you are included and important, you will be in conflict with your subconscious, which will say, "That's not true." Since we don't like to go against our beliefs, we will continue to believe that we are alone. Therefore, it is important to change your inner dialogue.

In Chapter 3, you learned about crushing the ANTs (automatic negative thoughts) and creating constructive anchor thoughts. There is a difference between anchor thoughts and affirmations. With affirmations, we can sometimes set a standard we cannot live up to, and that can make us feel even worse. For example, when we affirm with "I am successful" or "I am fantastic," the subconscious can say, "No, you are not." The claims feel false and untrue. We can create and be almost anything in life but not by lying to ourselves. If you tell yourself a statement that you don't actually agree with, you know deep inside that it is not true. Your subconscious will reject the lie, which leads to an internal conflict, and there is a risk that you will feel emotionally weaker than before you started affirming.

You need to have a supportive, encouraging, and praising inner dialogue. I remember Anna, a young girl I worked with, who didn't understand why she didn't win in swimming competitions, even though she trained hard. During our session, Anna experienced what it felt like when her swim coach pushed her to perform better and train harder. His choice of words was not always the best. Anna's inner dialogue became more and more negative about her performance, and she criticized herself harshly when she failed to reach her goals. Her swim coach had moved into her head.

If you have a "swim" coach in your head, one who pushes you into a negative thought pattern, you risk giving up instead of being inspired. You need to be a good friend to yourself. If you consider that you have a small child inside you who needs encouragement, support, and praise, you may not be as hard on yourself.

I MADE A MISTAKE

Major causes of the feeling of loneliness are guilt and shame. Guilt, to feel you have done something wrong, is a common emotion that I encounter in my work. Guilt can arise when, for example, we violate our code of honor, our moral code, or the values we follow to feel good about ourselves. Then we begin to feel shame—that there is something wrong with us, that we are not good, and that we are not worthy to feel good. *I haven't been good, so I get no reward.*

I meet clients who carry guilt that is ten, twenty, and sometimes, forty years old. It may be small things that still bother them. Stealing money from their mom's wallet, pushing their little brother, lying about eating the missing cookies, or not helping a friend.

Problems may also arise when an adult leaves a child to deal with guilt and shame on his or her own. The child might have to go to his room and stay there until he behaves properly. A child cannot sort everything that has happened out nor process the experience alone, but instead, sits there by himself with his guilt and shame. The child needs an adult who makes everything right and tells the child that he is loved. If this doesn't happen, the guilt and shame can be stored, planting the first seed for bad self-esteem.

We don't need to worry if we feel a sting of guilt when we have violated our moral code of honor or done wrong. Problems arise when we feel guilt that is not productive or if we hold on to guilt for a long time. The shame begins to erode our self-esteem. We often blame ourselves for a long time for something we did a long time ago. Performance anxiety, dissatisfaction, and perfectionism can be based on the feeling that we must balance our guilt. Unfortunately, the blame never seems to be resolved, and we have to constantly improve ourselves, do better, and be better. Whether the guilt is large or small, old or new, it is important to resolve the guilt.

I AM NOT OKAY

A deeper guilt and shame can arise when we feel that some parts of our personality are not okay. Since we cannot physically push them away, we instead create a split in order to have community with others. It may sound strange, but let me explain with an example.

You are having a cup of coffee at work with your colleague, Susanne. Another colleague, Lena, passes by. The boss has just delegated a number of exciting new tasks to Lena, which you really wanted to have but didn't dare ask for. You are disappointed that you didn't dare to ask your boss and are jealous of Lena because she now has more stimulating tasks than you have. You whisper to Susanne: "I wonder how she got the job? She doesn't have any special qualifications." You push Lena away, creating a split in the team, to get closer to Susanne.

This kind of alienation is something we can also create within ourselves.

CLIENT STORY

Why Are You Not Like Your Sister?

Peter's dream was to become one of the world's most successful stockbrokers. To get there, he needed to have a lot of energy, take risks, and make calculated, smart moves. To run with the big players, Peter had to be more forward, his boss said. Peter was aware that he often sat in the back seat and didn't dare to express himself. He wanted to change that.

Peter had a little sister who was a few years younger than he. As a kid, his sister could sit for hours playing with her dolls.

Peter was full of energy and rarely sat still. He was mischievous and inventive. His parents often sighed and said, "Why can't you be like your sister?" or "You need to calm down." From his parents' perspective, it was sometimes difficult to handle their son, who was full of energy and creativity. It was probably easier parenting a child who sat still and played quietly by herself. What the parents didn't understand was how their comments shaped Peter's self-image and what he later allowed himself to be. What sometimes fatigued the parents was just the very personality trait that could lead Peter to run with the big players in his professional life.

Adults often put blame on their children without thinking about it. *What will the neighbors say? You make me disappointed. You can do better. Why don't you do as I say? If you love me, you will do this for me.* These comments make children feel like something is wrong with them, and they must act in a certain way to be loved. Children want to be loved by their parents and do whatever it takes to earn that love. In Peter's case, his parents didn't have bad intentions; they probably just wanted peace and quiet and for their son to be perceived as well behaved. However, Peter interpreted it differently—*I'm annoying, I'm not okay as I am.* This becomes a threat to intimacy, community, and love and, thus, threatens the survival of the child.

When Peter's parents praised his sister as a role model, they unconsciously pushed Peter away. A fragmentation of the self occurs. Peter pushes away what his parents dislike to create closeness and community with them. Our minds can be divided into different parts, and we often push away the traits that are not accepted by our surroundings. This is how we create an internal split. As we grow up, some of our traits become dominant, and these traits are often more socially correct. Each time Peter tried to be more forward and take initiative, he felt the split, the trait he had to push aside to get his parents' approval. He was ashamed of the energy-rich and inventive part of himself and chose instead to sit in the back seat and avoid different situations.

Some of us can't satisfy our parents no matter what we do. In this case, there can only be one explanation—I am the problem. Almost all children blame themselves for the problems in their environment. We create split after split after split. Almost all of the parts inside us have become enemies. This creates an inner judgment, which can eventually lead to us feeling ashamed; there is nothing good about who we are. No matter how hard we tried, we couldn't split ourselves enough to create closeness and community with our parents. In the end, we lost ourselves. We only have a few traits left that we are allowed to show to the outside world. We feel shame before ourselves—incomplete, lonely, and worthless.

When we belittle ourselves in this way, we become lonely. Between yourself and the part you push away, a space is created . . . a separation, loneliness. The more parts of yourself that you push away, the more alone you feel. The further away you relegate your parts, the greater your loneliness. When you are separated within yourself, this is also how you experience your surroundings. You feel distanced from others and alone.

When we feel lonely, we want to quench that feeling because loneliness hurts. Working too much, smoking, drinking, shopping, betting on horses, or rushing through life are different ways of trying to escape the feeling of loneliness. I have even worked with clients who felt their cigarettes were their only friends—always there, rain or shine, never judging or demanding anything. The solution is to start facing yourself and who you really are. To become your own best friend.

YODA MOMENT

How our inner dialogue sounds and how many parts of ourselves we have pushed aside can create inner loneliness. We criticize and judge ourselves, and we lock parts of ourselves in the closet because we are ashamed of them. We are lonely because our inner team is not good enough and cannot participate. Here are some questions to explore your friendship with yourself:

- What do you say to yourself?
- What could you say to support and encourage yourself?
- What are your two top basic human needs?
- How do you meet your basic human needs today?

- Can you meet your basic human needs in a more constructive way?
- Are there situations in your life where you feel you have done wrong and are therefore not worth feeling good? "There will be no reward."
- What parts of yourself are you ashamed of?
- Who or what has caused you to feel ashamed and push these parts away?
- Would it be dangerous to view any of the parts you pushed away when you were a child?
- If a part is "annoying" or "wrong," did it have any purpose when it was created?
- If you have hidden certain parts from the outside world, how has it affected your life?
- If you keep hiding these parts, how do you think it will affect your life in the future?
- What advantages can you see that your hidden parts created in different situations?

JEDI MIND TRICKS

In order to heal loneliness and feel community, both with yourself and others, it is important that you understand and accept all of your parts and see their value. Encourage and praise yourself as you would with a toddler. And most importantly, dare to receive positivity and love.

⊶ HACK #22

HELLO FRIEND!

When you feel alone in your environment, this often reflects how it feels inside of you, between the different parts of yourself. Your parts are isolated from each other. To feel community with yourself and others, you need to face the parts you are ashamed of and that you have pushed away. But how do you actually do that?

Let's take one example. You have a loud part within you, and people often point out to you that you are a bit too loud. You begin to quiet down, and the needs of the loud part of your personality are not met. This is when the suppressed part can begin to emerge and create drama in unwanted situations.

Instead of judging and pushing away the loud side of you, allow it. I don't mean that you should be loud just about everywhere and all the time, but don't be ashamed of it. Allow it to come out every now and then: on the dance floor, at the football stadium, or during a lively debate. You can also ask that part why it's there, and discover its purpose—why it was created. Maybe you just needed to be heard? You can then give yourself permission to be heard, for example, by sharing ideas during meetings, singing in a choir, or talking about how you feel in a particular situation. When you do this, the loud voice may not have to hijack you randomly and loudly declare things. When you meet the needs of your suppressed parts, they begin to express themselves with less drama.

Allow yourself to get to know each part, and let them take space again. What are the different parts trying to do for you or protect you from? Think of all your parts as a team, where everyone has a function. All parts are important and everyone is needed on the team. Of course, at different times and in different doses, but no part is unnecessary, wrong, or wants to sabotage you. They just want to be involved. What positions in your team can you offer to the parts that were previously pushed away? Understanding, loving, and accepting ourselves is part of healing loneliness. We can never be whole unless we bring home all of our parts. To become more real and authentic, it's important that we begin to own and care for all of ourselves.

Accepting all your parts takes time. When we meet our hidden parts, both the pain around what we have had to push away and the fear of consequences if we show these sides of ourselves, are often aroused. If it feels a little uncomfortable when you start showing your hidden parts, you are probably on the right track. See yourself as a diamond. To sparkle, the diamond needs many facets, and so do you. The more facets you affirm, the more you sparkle. Both you and life become more exciting.

O—ᴛ HACK #23

GUILT SANITATION

A good way to clear out old guilt is to deal with people and situations where you know you should have acted differently. What do you need to sort out and fix? Who do you have a score to settle with and what misunderstandings do you need to sort out? Is there guilt and bad conscience that you can let go of? Is there someone you can say sorry to, or is there a promise you didn't keep that gives you a bad conscience? What do you need to say to these people?

Taking care of your old guilt can also mean forgiving yourself. Look at why you did "wrong" and if what you did really was wrong. Can you feel empathy for yourself? Sharing your story with someone who doesn't judge you can also help you heal.

Letting go of guilt creates relief, and our emotional cramp is diminished. We feel prouder of ourselves and build up our self-esteem.

O⊸ HACK #24

KEEP IN TOUCH

If an adult neglected us as children, we can find it difficult to understand as an adult that someone can like us or care about us. We don't think it matters whether we call our friends or not, whether we attend the party or not. We don't think anyone needs or misses us. We pull away and loneliness comes creeping in. What we don't think about is that we hurt others when we don't show interest in them. We may have difficulty understanding that people care about us, and they will be hurt when we disappear from their lives.

The cure is to keep in touch, even if you don't think you are important. Say yes to invitations.

O⊸ HACK #25

CREATE YOUR OWN POWER MANTRA

Since affirmations sometimes contain no action and are just a claim that you or something is good, there's not much effect. For something to change, you must be active. Create affirmations or mantras, defining what it is you should do and how to do it.

Examples

- I walk thirty minutes every day to make my body strong. I feel satisfied and proud of myself because I keep my promises to myself.
- I save thirty dollars each month so in one year, I can attend the medita-

tion course that will improve my life.

- I get up at 6:00 a.m. every day to do my morning rituals and create success in my life.
- Every time I do something good, I praise myself.

When you create a positive statement, a mantra, it is important that you don't go against your own belief system because it won't work as well. Choose a mantra that is meaningful to you, that opens you up to new opportunities, and is possible for you to fulfill right now. Your mantra should be like a beacon that keeps you on the right track.

Choose one goal or direction and one associated mantra at a time. If you have many goals, directions, and steps you want to address at the same time, it's like renovating the entire house at the same time. You start fixing something in every room, but nothing ever gets finished. When you multitask, you are less efficient, and this also applies to your goals.

Repeat your mantra frequently, preferably every day and sometimes several times a day. Charge your mantra with emotions, as positive emotions teach your body how your goal feels before you have achieved it, and your body becomes more willing to move forward. Count 5-4-3-2-1-GO and get started and do what you need to do. If a mantra doesn't work, it is often due to one of the following reasons:

- Your goal is too big or your action is too demanding. Break it down into smaller parts.
- Your goal or direction is not inspiring enough. Find a new goal or follow the energy, something you will learn more about in Chapter 10.
- You don't think you are worthy of success and feeling good, or you don't believe you can achieve your goal. Work on your inner dialogue or go to a coach/therapist who can help strengthen your belief in yourself.

O🔑 HACK #26

DARE TO RECEIVE

Gifts, help, and attention are signs of love. Many of us find it difficult to receive love in various forms, whether from ourselves, others, or the Universe. I often meet people who say they ask for help from the Universe, but when a friend tries to help them, they turn them down. If you cannot receive something from another human being, you cannot receive from the Universe. The reason is often that we have experienced conditional love, we have been hurt, and our trust is lost. There is no way around it: you have to start opening the door to your heart. Begin receiving small things, such as help with your heavy suitcase, a friendly hug, or a compliment.

CHAPTER 7 IN 60 SECONDS

- When you are afraid of being judged, you hide. You don't give people the opportunity to get to know you properly, and you become lonely.

- Guilt and shame create an internal split. You push away the parts that are not accepted by your surroundings. The separation inside you makes you feel alone.

- Working too much, smoking, drinking, shopping, betting on horses, or rushing through life are different ways of trying to run away from the feeling of loneliness.

- **Hello friend!** Get to know every part of yourself, and let them take their place. What are your different parts trying to do for you? All parts are important, and everyone is needed on the team.

- **Guilt sanitation.** Deal with people and situations where you should have acted differently. Forgive yourself for the mistakes you have made.

- **Stay in touch.** Get in touch with family, friends, and acquaintances. Say yes to their invitations.

- **Create your own power mantra.** Create a mantra that contains action and becomes your beacon to keep you on the right track.

- **Dare to receive.** All positive actions aimed at you are signs of love. Open the door to your heart and dare to receive.

CHAPTER 8

SLOW DOWN TO SPEED UP

If you slow down from time to time, you can improve your brainpower in just eight weeks. It is in stillness that you find your deeper intelligence.

I magine speeding on the highway. You know your final destination but need to follow the road signs to turn at the correct exit. The signs swish by. Suddenly, you stop. What did that road sign say? Didn't it say . . .?

In order to see the signs and the information, you need to slow down. Your intuition is like a road sign that swishes by, and to avoid missing it, you need to lower the speed. Slowing down is an effective way of creating internal control, gaining more clarity and focus, reducing fear, and becoming more creative and balanced. I like the phrase "you need to slow down to speed up."

That's just how I work with my clients. I help them slow down so they can accelerate their progress. I help them slow down to speed up when needed. As you slow down, you go from a state of high brain waves, where you are in survival mode, to a state of slow brain waves, where you are clear-thinking and solution-focused.

As you regularly slow down your brain waves, you train yourself to maintain this condition for longer and longer periods. You can be more balanced and use your brain capacity better. You make better decisions, see more opportunities, become more creative, focus better, and get things done faster. You become more stable in your mood and react in a better way; you become more motivated to do things and have more energy. All you have to do is slow down regularly and take a deep breath or two.

WHY DON'T WE SLOW DOWN?

Sometimes, we view ourselves as successful and significant when we are busy. We think we are efficient and in control. But being busy doesn't mean you are productive or that you are in control. In my work as a coach, I notice that many people are afraid to slow down. When we stop, we see ourselves and our behavior more clearly. We might need to confront where we are in life and roll up our sleeves to make a change. As we slow down, the truth tends to come to the surface, and we become more honest with ourselves. We remove distractions and focus on what is important. It can be scary to face what we are trying to run away from: ourselves, our problems, our doubts, our pain, and life, in general. The problem with constantly sprinting is that the brain gets tired. We become overwhelmed and go into survival mode, finding it harder to see opportunities and the best solutions.

Many of us wait for something to happen, such as illness, death, dismissal from work, or a broken relationship, before we create change. Why wait? You can learn and change your life based on curiosity, joy, and inspiration instead of pain and suffering.

THE BRAIN TAKES A SMOKE BREAK

The brain uses ingenious ways to help us unwind. Postponing things can be a way for the brain to take a break. If we are constantly stressed—for example, over the economy, our children, or our self-esteem, we make the brain tired. So when we are at work and see the to-do list, the brain says, "I have already worried for hours about everything. I can't cope anymore. Let's take a break." You go online and watch cute animal videos, shop, or just surf around. Suddenly, an hour has passed. Postponing things is not always about lack of discipline or having taken on too great a goal; it can be caused by too much worry in your life. Your brain simply needs a "smoke break." The stress triggers you, and the strategy you use to avoid it is to postpone things. In the end, it has become a habit to handle stress that way. Instead, try to resolve the underlying turmoil, and don't be too hard on yourself. Do something small that you can handle. Decide to take five minutes and do a few things on the list. Most often, the start is the most difficult part. Studies show that once we get started, 80 percent of us will continue.

OUR BRAIN WAVES

Before I explain how you can slow down your brain, I want to explain how the different brain waves work. Our brain consists of nerve cells that communicate with each other by means of electrical impulses. These electrical impulses, which travel through our neurons, are called brain waves, and they have specific functions. The five brain frequencies are:

Delta

Between birth and up to the age of two, our brain works in delta, the slowest brain waves. Babies are controlled by the subconscious and hardly any information that comes from outside is edited. There is no critical, analytical thinking or judgment. The conscious part of the brain operates at a low level. Tibetan monks who have meditated for decades can reach this level in an alert, awake state while typical adults only reach it when we are asleep.

Theta

Between about two and six years of age, brain activity increases, and children enter the theta brain waves state. A child fantasizes a lot and lives in his inner world. A young child doesn't think logically or rationally and accepts most of what you say to them. The programming is in full swing: "Money doesn't grow on trees; boys don't cry; you can't do that." The child's subconscious mind is wide open for information, and the focus is on one's own feelings.

When children discover their feelings change, they begin to associate this phenomenon with what is happening outside themselves. The brain takes snapshots of what happens in the environment when a particular emotion arises. In this way, children pick up what it is that makes them feel good or bad or feel in a certain way . . . and what caused it. This helps them navigate in the best way to avoid pain, feel safe, and be accepted.

As an adult, we can reach the theta state when we meditate or are in hypnosis. We move from our logical thinking to a deeper state of consciousness with stronger intuition, more capacity to solve complex problems, greater ability to visualize, and a sense of wholeness. It is in theta brain waves that I mostly work with my clients to create fast results. In this state, the hard drive opens, we get in contact with the subconscious, and we access the information more easily to make changes.

Alpha

Between the ages of about six and twelve, children enter the state of alpha brain waves. Around the age of six to nine, the analytical part of the brain begins to evolve gradually. A child begins to interpret experiences and draw conclusions, although the imagination and the inner world are still important. When we experience alpha brain waves as an adult, our thinking slows down, and we feel calmer, more peaceful, and more grounded. After yoga class, a walk in nature, or a massage, we are often in this alpha state. We reflect and dream away. Our two brain halves are more in balance.

Beta

From about the age of twelve, a child's brain enters a state of beta brain waves. Analytical, logical thinking develops further. The door between the conscious (the thinking brain) and the subconscious (the programming and the imagination) begins to close. As an adult, the beta state is our everyday state. We are alert and the thinking, conscious part of our brains analyze, plan, assess, and categorize.

Gamma

Gamma brain waves are associated with super focus, high mental and physical ability, and feelings of happiness. Neuroscientists believe the gamma waves can link information from all parts of the brain and that many brain cells are fired simultaneously. Your brain and body are in sync. You are "in the zone." People with high levels of gamma activity are exceptionally intelligent, have great compassion, and strong self-control. Elite athletes, world-class performers, and high achievers in all areas produce more gamma brain waves than usual.

The benefits of producing more gamma brain waves are:

- Better memory.
- Your five senses (sight, hearing, touch, taste, and scent) become more sensitive. Your experiences become richer, and you pick up more information from your surroundings.
- Sharper focus.
- Your brain can process more information faster.
- Increased feelings of happiness, joy, calm, and satisfaction.
- Increased creativity.
- Greater self-control.

The gamma frequency is activated when, among other things:

- During your REM sleep—the period when you dream, and the brain's nerve cells have the same level of activity as when you are awake.
- During visualization, as you learned in Chapter 3.
- When you meditate, especially if you focus on the heart and a sense of gratitude, compassion, and love. Studies show that when monks meditate with focus on the heart, they exhibit gamma waves.

In this chapter you will learn meditation, or self-hypnosis as it is also called, which will help you use more of your brain capacity. You will be able to reduce activity in the amygdala, the brain's fight-or-flight center, and become smarter, happier, calmer, and more balanced as the weeks go by.

DIFFERENT BRAIN WAVES FOR DIFFERENT NEEDS

We use different clothes in different weather conditions. Simplified, it is the same with brain waves. They are used for a variety of purposes.

GAMMA – when you need to be in "the zone." Most of us would probably like to be in this state all the time, but it is not a permanent state.

BETA – as an adult you are in the beta state most of the day. It is your everyday state of mind where you are alert and aware of the outside world. The thinking part of the brain is active. Here, logic, analytical ability, reason, willpower, and intention are strong. The conscious mind accounts for about 5 percent of your total mind while the subconscious, with all your programming, accounts for about 95 percent.

ALPHA – when you close your eyes, data collection from the outside world decreases by as much as 80 percent. You analyze less, and your inner world becomes clearer. Stress and anxiety decrease, and you feel more relaxed. Your brain hits the pause button. The moments when you stare out into nothingness, you are having an alpha moment.

THETA –more of a dream state, even though you are awake. The door between the conscious and the subconscious is open, and you gain insights, becoming more creative and solution oriented. You are susceptible to change and growth.

DELTA –where you sleep deeply with very little awareness. Here your brain gets to rest. In this state, repair and recovery takes place.

Three Levels of Beta

We spend most of our waking time in the beta state, and our focus is on our external environment. Our conscious part of the brain is busy processing, analyzing, and storing all of the information that comes from the outside world through our five senses. Our emotional part of the brain provides us with emotions based on the incoming information—how we should feel about what we experience.

We can divide the beta brain waves into three levels:

1. Slow beta waves – you're attentive but still quite relaxed. Much like when you enjoy reading a good book.

2. Medium beta waves – you are more focused, attentive, and analyze more. Your logic switch is switched on. For example, when you learn something new.

3. High beta waves – stress hormones are produced in your body. When you are emotional, upset, scared, impatient, stressed, irritated, or judgmental, you are in high beta. You are extra vigilant, worried, and over-focused. Your brain is excited. You stop thinking and instead, feel and react. You have a harder time focusing and solving problems because you are hyper. You can even over-focus and become so obsessed with something that it becomes difficult for you to stop. It is good to be able to focus in a dangerous or stressful situation, where we need to get the job done, but if we stay in these high brain waves for too long, it will eventually cause imbalance in the body. We are drained of energy and become tired, anxious, depressed, obsessed, indecisive, scared, and competitive. We cannot relax or fall asleep. This is not the state where we learn something new, open our hearts, or trust our own abilities.

You have use for all of your brain waves, depending on what you want to achieve. Delta is good for resting and repairing. Theta when you want to be creative and solution oriented. Alpha to release worry and stress. Beta to be attentive and aware of your surroundings, as well as for analysis and logic. In emergency situations, high beta waves may also be needed.

However, if you stay in the high beta state for much of the day, it is not good. This is only meant for emergencies, when survival is a priority. Being constantly in survival mode affects your entire system. When you try to analyze, be creative, and solve problems in this state, things don't go very well. In the high brain waves, stress chemicals are produced that get the brain off balance. When our thinking part of the brain doesn't work optimally, it creates imbalance in our nervous system and a chaos of emotions arises. We become very focused on our external world—people, things and situations—and we become problem-focused rather than solution-focused. We see the bad more than the good. We lock ourselves and find it difficult to learn and absorb new information. Our inner GPS strikes, and it gets hard to know who we are or where we want to go in life. Our survival is a priority. It is difficult to grow and change when the body is stressed. The brain just wants to find quick solutions to escape the stress; it doesn't have the time or energy for more long-term projects or curiosity about new things.

When you are in high beta waves for an extended period of time, you tear apart your inner system. Both your cognitive and emotional functions in the brain are affected:

- Your memory deteriorates, and you find it harder to think clearly and focus. The brain can feel like syrup, and you can't solve problems or bring in new knowledge as well. If you feel stupid, unfocused, or forgetful, you may be in the high beta state too often.
- You get tunnel vision. It becomes difficult to make decisions, and you find it harder to see opportunities and find creative solutions.
- You get tired and lack energy, or you feel hyper.
- You become sensitive to sounds, lights, and smells.
- You become unbalanced in your mood and your emotions.
- You become depressed, and nothing feels fun anymore.
- Your experience fear and anxiety increases. You may have physical reactions, such as palpitations, shortness of breath, sweating, stomach pain, or pressure over the chest.
- The risk is you will start using some kind of drug or distraction to unwind your brain. For example, food, alcohol, cigarettes, exercise, or shopping.

 ## YODA MOMENT
- How often do you think you are in the high beta brain wave state?
- How do you think it affects your life?
- What could you do to slow down your brain waves?

JEDI MIND TRICKS

Self-hypnosis is a way to slow down the brain and body so your entire system starts to work better. You move from the sympathetic nervous system to the parasympathetic. From survival to living. Self-hypnosis is one of the most effective tools for controlling your thoughts and experiencing more peace, clarity, and joy in life. When you learn to be in the alpha and theta state, you give your body rest that is five times deeper than when you sleep. You soothe your nervous system and release stress from the body while also buffering energy, which increases your productivity. Your thoughts become more open, creative, and relaxed. This is what your brain prefers.

Difference Between Meditation and Self-Hypnosis

Meditation and hypnosis are two different belief systems that describe the same state of mind—a state in which you are completely focused on your inner world and can view yourself, come to conclusions, and grow. Meditation is a way to go into a hypnotic state, where you can get past the analytical mind, slow down the brain waves, and access the operating system, your subconscious mind, your matrix, and create change. Hypnosis is a natural condition you experience every day. When you wake up and fall asleep, you pass hypnosis, that is, the alpha and theta states.

Get Mentally Strong

When we control our mind, we increase our mental strength, flexibility, efficiency, and emotional intelligence. Neuroscientist Sara Lazar discovered that meditation increases the gray matter in the brain, which contains billions of nerve cells that send impulses back and forth and make us think, act, and react. The most exciting discovery was that those who meditated for a long time had more gray matter in the prefrontal cortex, our executive part of the brain. Most people's prefrontal cortex shrinks with age, but the fifty-year-old meditators had the same amount of gray matter as the twenty-five-year-olds. Lazar did another study that found that only eight weeks of meditation was needed to improve brain capacity. Learning, memory function, and emotion regulation were improved. The ability to see things from different perspectives and show empathy was strengthened, and the amygdala—which is linked to fear, anxiety, and aggression—shrank. It is in silence that we find our wisdom and deeper intelligence.

The more you exercise your ability to be in the alpha and theta brain wave states, the longer you can stay in a balanced state during the day, even if you are exposed to the effects of your surroundings. You become stronger and more capable. And even if you can't hypnotize away all of the problems, such as an idiotic manager or a bad relationship, the self-hypnosis makes you stronger and wiser. You see more clearly what you need so you can make better decisions. You gain power so that you can change what doesn't work in your life.

O⎯⊤ HACK #27

UNWIND

The first step to unwind is to learn self-hypnosis. That is when the door between the conscious and the subconscious opens. What sets them apart is the analytical mind. As you get past the analytical mind, you become more open to new ideas, to relearning, and to letting go of what doesn't work. One can say that the analytical mind is the gatekeeper who decides which new ideas should be approved and admitted. If you have an analytical mind that is negative and firm in its opinions, it will not let anything new in. Some move easily past the analytical mind and into the subconscious; others have a thicker wall. When you're in beta brain waves and over-analyzing, you move further away from the operating system, your matrix, where you can create change. You need to slow down the brain waves to access the operating system in the subconscious and affect your programs. There are several studies that show that after eight weeks, you can see positive changes with only fifteen to twenty minutes of meditation/self-hypnosis per day.

Here are some tips to succeed with your self-hypnosis:

- There are two times a day when the subconscious mind is more open, and it is easier to relax and reach the slower brain waves. Directly in the morning when you wake up—because then you have just passed alpha and theta—and in the evening because your brain is tired and preparing for sleep. Feel free to do your self-hypnosis at any of these times.
- Do self-hypnosis once or twice a day, if possible. Preferably the same time each day, so that in the end, it becomes a routine.
- Make sure you are undisturbed. Notify the family and turn off the sound on your mobile phone.
- Use earplugs and a sleeping mask if you want to turn off sound and light.

- If possible, choose a specific location for your self-hypnosis. The place soon becomes associated with relaxation and when you sit there, the brain will have an easier time focusing inward. You can also decorate the place with a candle, flowers, or similar things if they feel right for you.
- Don't do your self-hypnosis lying down or sitting in bed because your bed is linked to sleep. You can sit in a chair, armchair, cross-legged on the floor, or on a comfortable pillow. Sit with straight back and relaxed arms and legs.
- If you choose to have some kind of background music, choose something meditative and that soothes your body. I switch between having my environment completely quiet and some kind of soft, spiritual music.
- Close your eyes and take a few deep breaths. Shift your focus inward. When you close your eyes, you eliminate the amount of light that enters your eyes, which slows down your brain waves automatically as your brain chemistry slows down. When you close your eyes, you reduce incoming information by up to 80 percent. As you breathe deeper, you relax more. When you take in fewer impressions from the surroundings, your inner world becomes clearer, and you notice more easily your thoughts and feelings.
- Start by going into self-hypnosis for five minutes. Then gradually increase to about twenty minutes or longer, if you wish.
- In the beginning, you might nod off; it is quite natural. It is the body that relaxes. After a while, you will get used to being completely relaxed and still able to sit with your back straight.
- At first, you may feel that your thoughts are swirling around in your head, and you feel restless. It's a sign that you are in high beta state and need to teach your body and brain to relax. If you can't relax and meditate without being too restless, it may be good to know that it is your survival instinct that is haunting you. We are not coded to close our eyes and relax when we are in survival mode. It's not the right time for this when trying to survive.
- You will have good and less good hypnosis moments. Some days, you will be able to relax faster and more easily quiet your thoughts. Other days,

you will experience a busy highway up there, but just keep going. After a few weeks, you will notice small positive changes—more calmness, clarity, and balance.

If You Have a Hard Time Relaxing

If you have trouble relaxing and slowing down your thoughts, you can start by focusing on different body parts. It shuts down your analytical mind and helps you experience emotions and sensations. Emotions are the body's language and by focusing on different body parts, you think less. For example, you can scan your body, from your head down to your feet. You stop at each part of the body for a while and imagine the space that each part occupies and how it feels. Then you experience your body as a whole and imagine the body surrounded by space or void. You become something more than your body, and you may experience how you begin to float out of your body, hover above it, and view it from above.

Neuroscientist Joe Dispenza begins his meditations in this way. Dispenza and his team have created a formula they use to scientifically measure any increase of the coherency of the brain. Dispenza means that when we focus on an object or thing, we narrow our focus, just as when we are stressed. We focus on matter. The quantum model, on the other hand, says that reality has both particle and wave properties, both matter and energy. When we instead focus on space and void, we open our awareness. We reach beyond matter and can gain access to the quantum field, the energy, and the endless possibilities. As we feel and experience the void, we think less and begin to slow down the brain waves. When we don't think, we stop analyzing. When we stop analyzing, we open the door to the subconscious, the operating system, where we can change. When we feel the void, we connect with the limbic system and get in touch with the autonomic nervous system, whose job is to create coherency and balance. The autonomic nervous system, in turn, connects with the conscious mind and creates order and clarity in the brain.

Another way to train your nervous system to become more resilient is through HRV training and Firstbeat. Search on Google for it. These tools help you easily measure how your system responds to stress and what you need to do to restore balance to your nervous system. Trained tutors can be found around the world.

O—ᴛ HACK #28

MAKE A BRAIN DUMP

When you feel overwhelmed by what is happening in your life, you need to slow down. When your brain is overheated, it's because there is too much happening inside it. The brain is filled with so much information that it eventually overflows with everything that needs to be done. This can create anxiety. It becomes harder to focus, and you end up running around without getting anything done. Time for a brain dump!

Get the paper and pencil out and dump everything you think about. Write down everything you worry about not catching up with and everything you need to do—basically everything you're thinking about. Once you have written everything down, highlight the three most important things you need to do for something concrete to happen and for you to move toward what you want. Then make a circle around the most important thing, and do it first. Everything else on the list you remove, delegate, or do later. When I wrote this book, I struck cleaning time, blog posts, and a number of other things from my to-do list.

O—ᴛ HACK #29

BECOME AN EXPLORER

If you want to take another step, you can become an explorer in your own mind. Let's start with a quick rehearsal. Simply put, we can divide the brain into three parts:

The Conscious or Thinking Part

This part is called the neocortex and is the youngest part of our brain . . . and the most advanced. There is also the prefrontal cortex, our chief executive officer or command center, which helps us set direction and goals, gather information, plan, focus, make judgments, solve problems, make conscious choices, and take us forward. We use this part about 5 percent of the day.

Emotional Mind

This part is called the limbic system, the chemical brain, or the emotional brain. This part releases chemicals that affect the entire body. The limbic system helps us to form long-term memories because we can more easily remember the feeling or sensation that is linked to the experience than the factual information in the experience itself.

The Subconscious Mind

This part consists of the cerebellum and, together with the brain stem, is part of the reptile brain. Here, our habits, attitudes, and behaviors are stored. The subconscious automates everything we do, making life easier for us. Ninety-five percent of your thirty-five-year-old self is a set of memorized behaviors, emotional reactions, beliefs, perceptions, and attitudes. Your matrix controls 95 percent of your day. Because your subconscious stores so much information and programs and controls much of your day, you need to understand how it works. Trying to change the programs that have been running for many years with your conscious 5 percent is a difficult task. The key is instead to get into the subconscious where the operating system is. With self-hypnosis and slower brain waves, you can study your matrix, update the information, and direct your thoughts, feelings, and behaviors.

In self-hypnosis, when you don't think and analyze as much, you open up different parts of the brain. They start to synchronize with each other, and the brain becomes more coherent and you become smarter. You can more easily explore who you are and what you want to change as you reach the body's control center. You can choose to explore limiting feelings, habits, thoughts, behaviors, and beliefs that you want to change. Here is a technique I often use with my clients—and also which neuroscientist Joe Dispenza uses in his powerful meditations.

Start by asking a few questions before going into self-hypnosis.

- Who am I outward to the world, and who am I on the inside?
- What thoughts, feelings, behaviors, habits, or beliefs limit me in life?
- What do I want to change in my life?
- What do I need to work on to become or remain a person whom I like and am proud of?
- Who do I want to be?

- What am I grateful for?

Flowchart

1. **Work on one change at a time.** Choose a limiting thought, feeling, habit, behavior, or belief.

2. **Close your eyes and relax briefly.** Relaxation can be as simple as focusing on your breathing.

3. **Think about how you feel** when you have that limiting thought, feeling, habit, behavior, or belief. Notice the sensations in the body. Is the limitation in the body? Where? Experience the restriction as energy.

4. **Let the thought and feeling wander back in time.** How did this thought, feeling, habit, behavior, or belief come about? What have you experienced before in your life, which you have interpreted in a certain way and which today has become a strategy and ultimately part of your personality? Are these thoughts true, or are they just an echo of the past?

5. **Notice your thoughts.** What do you think about yourself or life? Dare to see the truth. It is said that our lives change in direct relation to how much truth about ourselves we can accept. To dare to see ourselves mentally and emotionally naked and accepting ourselves is sometimes difficult. We don't always want to know who we really are because what if we are not capable or loveable just as we are? Recognizing and communicating our fears to ourselves, another person, or the Universe gives relief. When you understand yourself better, you can more easily change patterns and move on. When you tear down your facade and get real, you make breakthroughs. When you let go of the fear, you let the negative energy move out of your system. You become FREE.

6. **Declare loudly to yourself who you have been until today.** Accept what you have denied, without judging. The thoughts, feelings, habits, behaviors, and beliefs. Declare what you want to let go of and let the energy be released. If you don't know how to let go or solve the problem, have confidence that the solution will come to you. Ask for help, and let the Universe do the rest. Don't just wish for it because that indicates there

is a lack of something or that you don't have the ability to take control of your situation.

7. **Observe yourself** in different situations where your limitation is reminded. Notice what program (habits) drives you, what triggers you (the cause), and the result (feelings). How do you think, feel, and act?

8. **Say STOP** to yourself.

9. **Visualize situations** where you act as the person you want to be, without limitations. Load the visualization with positive emotions.

10. **Think a thought of gratitude**, as if the change has already happened.

By regularly exploring yourself, you become aware of how you think, feel, and act during the day. You notice when your old programming shows up. This gives you control over your reactions and an opportunity to break old patterns. You are redirecting yourself from reacting unconsciously to creating conscious pathways in the brain. Finally, you react less to what previously affected you. This is how you step into your POWER and create FREEDOM.

By regularly visualizing, as you learned in Chapter 3, you can start building new pathways in the brain. Allow yourself to bathe in the feeling of being there already. Then, take small steps in harmony with the person you are in your visualization. Notice how your reality begins to change. The work you do within you will eventually be manifested in your outer world. Everything starts from the inside.

Loading your visualization with positive emotions is a very important component. If you think positively, such as "I can fix this," "I'm fine," or "I'm valuable" but still *feel* fear, dissatisfaction, or inadequacy, the thought will never pass through the brainstem and into the body because the thought is not in line with the body's emotional state. Thus, to make a radical change, you need to change your emotional state, and an effective way to do that is through gratitude.

Usually, we are grateful for something good that has already happened, but if we express gratitude as a regular habit, even before something has happened, and are grateful for what will come to us in the future, the body believes it is getting something today. The emotional signature of gratitude is that the positive has already happened. When you think positively in your self-hypnosis or visualization, you program the circuits in your brain to think in a way that is good for you. If you also load the experience with positive emotions, you will teach your body how your future feels before it happens, and your body becomes more willing to move into the future. Thoughts are the language of the brain and emotions are the language of the body. How you think and feel creates your inner state.

When it's bedtime, feel free to make a brief assessment of how you have acted during the day—whether it was in harmony with your visualization or if there was something you could do differently the next day. It will take some training and patience to change old thoughts, feelings, and behaviors, and you need to repeat, repeat, and repeat. This applies to all learning. When you need to change a habit or learn something new, you need to repeat it many times for it to be neurologically imprinted. Finally, it is activated in the third part of the brain, the cerebellum—also called the subconscious mind. What you do becomes automated, a habit or skill that you do without thinking or having to put in a lot of effort.

O⇁ HACK #30

EDIT YOUR STORY

When something doesn't go our way, it is easy to start focusing on what's not working, whose fault it is, why it went the way it did, and what could have been done instead.

Close your eyes and say to yourself:

- It didn't work because . . .
- I don't reach my potential because . . .
- I don't have a good life because . . .

What is your story or excuse? Is that a good excuse? Does it sound true? We often create a story that is not really true about why we are not where we should be in life. We use excuses to explain why we haven't achieved our goals.

Decide to adjust your story. What can you do to create the change you want? What positive experiences have come from your past experiences?

My story today is:

I am brave because my childhood taught me to venture out into unfamiliar territory. I've had to reprogram large parts of my thoughts and feelings; therefore, I'm not afraid to explore and learn new things. Since I learned early on how to take care of myself, today I am independent and make decisions for my life. This is POWER and FREEDOM for me.

How does your story sound?

CHAPTER 8 IN 60 SECONDS

- When you slow down regularly, you can use your brain capacity better.
- It only takes eight weeks to improve brain capacity.
- Being in a high brain wave state for too long produces stress that gets the brain off balance. You become problem-oriented rather than solution-focused. Your inner GPS goes on strike, and you lose the direction in life.
- **Unwind.** Learn self-hypnosis to unwind to a state of slower brain waves, so your system works better.
- **Make a brain dump.** Write down everything you are worried about not catching up with or managing and everything you need to do. Draw a circle around the most important thing you need to do for something concrete to happen, and do it first.
- **Become an explorer.** Explore who you are and what you want to change in your life by opening the door to your subconscious where all your programs are.
- **Edit your story.** What is your story or excuse for not being where you want in life? Decide to edit your story.

ACTIVATE YOUR GPS

*Your internal GPS is always active. It constantly provides
signals and information about how your route forward
hould look for you to grow and feel good.*

We all have an internal GPS that tells us what is right and wrong for
us, what we want and don't want. We can call this intuition, a gut
feeling, clarity, instinct, or inner wisdom. Answers and clarity come
from within, rarely from the outside.

CLIENT STORY

Something Is Not Right

Eva had been working at her job for a few months when she began
to feel as if something was wrong. She felt restless, exhausted,
and often sad but didn't understand why. This was her dream
job—a step up in her career, an interesting job, a higher salary,

and more responsibilities. "Something can't be wrong already. I've only been here for a few months," she thought. With the help of my coaching, she realized quite quickly that the workplace, the manager, nor the work tasks suited her. She really wanted to educate and inspire people, but that was a pretty small part of the job. So why had she chosen the job? She thought the title, money, increased responsibility, and the step up in her career were what she wanted. The insight landed with a bang. Status and money were important to her father, and she was still seeking his approval. She enjoyed meeting people, teaching, and inspiring. Eva understood that she should find a job where she got to do what she really enjoyed. Her inner GPS clearly stated that she had to leave her work, even if it meant a so-called setback in salary and prestige. The joy of the job was most important to her.

OUR GPS IS ALWAYS ACTIVE

Did you know the brain and stomach are formed from the same embryonic tissue in the uterus? After a while, the tissue divides, and one part forms the brain, while the other part forms the stomach. It is therefore quite natural to call the stomach our second brain. The same type of neurological pathways are found in the stomach and the brain. So our intuition or gut feeling is not hocus-pocus. The stomach is a very sophisticated instrument for collecting information and is usually correct. The gut feeling is based on an incredible amount of information, both from within and from our surroundings, which allows us to determine quickly whether something feels right or wrong. You probably recognize those "I just knew" moments, when you knew exactly what you needed to do and when something felt right, even if you didn't have that many facts to go on. You have also probably felt that strange sensation in your stomach when something was not right but kept going anyway, only to discover afterward that you should have backed off.

I remember when I was applying to a prestigious job that I wanted because of the assignments, the title, and the salary. Something didn't feel right in my stomach during the interviews and tests that I had to undergo. Did I listen? No.

I got the job and was happy for about two months, and then it hit me. The job was not at all as it had been presented to me, and the staff was acting stiff. I later understood this behavior came from a fear of making mistakes. The manager was controlling and manipulative. I felt bad, and my energy and joy dropped. I was disappointed. When I finally left the job, I felt such enormous relief. My GPS had alerted me when I had applied for the job and proved it was right when I quit. As I said before, your inner wisdom is usually correct.

Our wisdom is hard-coded in the body. Our body constantly gives us signals of what we need. If we need food, the body sends hunger signals, and the stomach growls. If we need sleep, the body sends the signal of fatigue and the bed becomes irresistible. There is nothing wrong with our signal system; it is just that we have stopped listening. Why is that the case?

It usually starts when we are young children. The adults tell us what to do and how to do things. There is nothing wrong with that, but if we don't teach children to think, choose, and try for themselves, they will lose contact with their internal GPS. Imagine a baby that is hungry. The baby cries and doesn't care if it's 02:00 a.m. When we grow up, it is not very convenient to eat at 2:00 in the morning; instead, we are guided to meal times that parents, Kindergarten, and later school schedules have decided. We stop listening to our inner food clock and adapt to society's schedule. Of course, it has to be so because it would be difficult to make life work if everyone ate at exactly the time they wanted. Now imagine . . . we do this in many areas!

We listen to parents, teachers, managers, authorities, experts, friends, family, and partners. We drown in information from others regarding what is right or wrong, good or bad, useful or useless, and smart or stupid. Until, one day, the signal from our GPS becomes so weak that we can no longer hear it. The times we hear it, we don't dare trust it. We haven't tested our GPS in a long time. What if we are wrong and everyone else is right?

Another example is when the child senses moods in the home, but the parents pretend the problem doesn't exist. Let's say that parents are not happy in their relationship. The child notices something is wrong, but no one talks about it. If the child asks, the parents might say that everything is okay. The child gets confused. "I feel something is not okay, but everyone says it's okay. What's right here? My GPS doesn't seem to be working, I'm probably wrong." The child stops following his gut feeling and waits for someone to tell him about what is right and wrong, what is real or not.

Our internal GPS is always active. It constantly gives signals and information about how our route ahead should look for us to feel good. The question is: can you hear your GPS? And if you hear your GPS, do you follow it?

UNDERSTAND YOUR SIGNALS

Did you know that your body gives you signals when you need to grow? Variation, development, and growth are basic human needs. When you are not developing, the body sends a signal, and you feel bored, stagnated, slow, powerless, or lost. That's when you should act. A sense of stagnation is a signal that you need to move on. It is your inner wisdom, saying, "Wake up! You need to investigate this; you need to change something."

Nothing is necessarily wrong when you feel bored, stagnated, slow, powerless, or lost. It's just a signal, a message that you need to change something and move forward. When we don't grow and experience variation in our lives, we become bored. When we live a life too ingrained, our brains can suddenly require variation, which may come as a surprise. An impulse we may not be able to control, as the need to break the boredom is like a pent-up tidal wave. This is what I call "the man at the conference with his tie around his head." I think you know who I mean. That person at a conference who does unthinkable things, which he or she is likely to regret the next day.

When something feels tedious, we lose energy, and it is a sign we need to change something. When I lose energy, I try the exclusion method. I remove things or people, or step out of situations and investigate what happens. It's a detective job. I'm always looking for clues. What happens to my energy if I reduce contact with a certain person, engaging in less activity or remove the relationship altogether? It may also be the reverse: that I must add something. Sometimes, it's hard to think of what gives us energy or drains us. We need a dose of patience.

Curiosity and positive energy are also signals. When something makes you curious or gives you energy, it's your GPS saying this is good for you and something you should do more of. Think of the signals as the oil light on your car's dashboard.

It lights up to give you information: You need to add oil so the engine is not damaged. Listen to your signals, and you will begin to understand them better.

I once worked with a woman who was depressed. She didn't understand why because she had a good life. She was thinking about getting divorced—maybe it was her husband who was wrong for her. It turned out that what she lacked in life was growth. She was bored and had run in the same track for many years. Her life didn't involve much fun. The realization that she needed to grow and that there was nothing wrong with either her relationship or life at large stopped her from making the wrong decision. Instead, she began to explore life and grow as a person. The depression disappeared.

When tracking your signals, clarity from your GPS is important. It helps you:

- Move faster and reach your goals easier because you are clear about where you want to go.
- Make better decisions and create a better life for yourself.
- See your next step in your projects and commitments.
- See what doesn't suit you, so you can change before it steals your joy and energy.
- Understand what needs drive you, so you get to know yourself better.
- Understand your habits, triggers, blockages, and reactions, so you can change them.

If you are afraid to follow your GPS, it may be because it has a tendency to challenge you to try new things, which may be scary. Your intuition may give you a signal to look for a new job, move to a new city, or talk to a person at a party. It wants to send you out into unfamiliar territory because that's where you grow, and it's exciting. Your inner guardian, whose job is to protect you from dangers, doesn't like growth and excitement. If you have a strong guardian, it can make you ignore what your GPS encourages you to do.

YODA MOMENT

Your instincts are worth their weight in gold. They know what's good, right, and important to you. Excuses hold you back. What slows you down? Fear, doubt, or being overwhelmed? Do you lack time, patience, money, opportunities, or energy? Reflect on what you know, but don't act yet. Being honest is an important part of creating clarity.

- Write down moments when you had clarity in your life, when you followed your GPS and "just knew."
- In what ways do you feel bored, stagnated, slow, powerless, or lost?
- In which areas of your life do you choose not to act?
- What are you putting off?
- What do you need to do to change or improve in your life, have more fun, feel better, and have more energy?
- What are you curious about?
- What do you get energy from?
- If you were not afraid, what would you do?
- What excuses do you use for not moving forward?

What Affects Your Inner State?

Many of us experience stress every day. We work, clean, shop, do the laundry, exercise, take care of our family, meet friends . . . Maybe we have a bad boss, a child who doesn't enjoy school, or a strained economy. We are bombarded daily with impressions from our surroundings and media in various forms. Internal concerns can also stress us: the inability to manage things, not find solutions, fail, think the future will not be as we want. Concerns are like weeds. They grow and spread to other areas, and suddenly we are worried about almost everything. Worrying is a habit that is often rooted early on; it may start by living with a worried parent, experiencing situations we have not been able to control, or dealing with things we couldn't handle. In those moments, we felt small and helpless. This can create a general sense of anxiety later in life. The brain likes to worry because it creates a feeling that it is actually doing something. Unfortunately, it is an illusion since nothing concrete is happening.

Stress, anxiety, and the constant influx of impressions create chaos in the body and make it very difficult for you to create clarity and hear your inner GPS. The hippocampus, the part of the brain where your memories are handled, shrinks from stress, and this also affects your clarity. When I worked very hard for a period, there were days when I couldn't even make small or simple decisions. My clarity was gone.

Stress affects the nervous system. We have two different nervous systems, which are part of the whole system, which function as your inner GPS—the sympathetic nervous system and the parasympathetic nervous system. If we start with the sympathetic nervous system, we can simply say it is activated in situations where you are exposed to mental or physical stress. It activates your fight-or-flight function and prepares your body for action. When we are stressed and bombarded with impressions, the sympathetic nervous system is triggered and we are always a little tense, or "on the edge." If you often feel tired, unmotivated, anxious, drained, or disconnected, your sympathetic nervous system may be overloaded. Your body works against you, and it becomes difficult to create clarity and connect with your inner GPS. Instead, you need to activate the parasympathetic system, which lets you unwind and recover. The vagus nerve is an important part of this system and needs to be stimulated to get you in balance.

The Body's Air Traffic Controller

The vagus nerve is the body's air traffic controller and has control over most of what happens in your body. It is the longest nerve of the body, which actually consists of two separate nerve paths that run from the brain stem to the intestine and which connects the brain with all the important organs in the body. It knows how you and your internal organs are feeling and what needs to be done. The vagus nerve has over 80,000 nerve threads that control various processes and is involved in almost everything that happens in your body. It has an overview of everything going on in the body, while also communicating with the brain about how to solve any problems in the best way. The role of the vagus nerve is to mediate between body, thoughts, and emotions. It is responsible for turning off the fight-or-flight reflex and creating recovery and relaxation. The vagus nerve can also be the single most important component of your body when it comes to creating peace, happiness and complete balance. Did you know that both the stomach and the heart communicate with the brain via the vagus nerve? So when we say, "trust your gut" or "listen to your heart," we really mean that we should listen and trust our vagus nerve.

How your vagus nerve works can be inherited from mother to child. Mothers who are depressed, angry, or anxious during pregnancy have lower activity in their vagus nerve, which can be passed on to the child who may experience low dopamine and serotonin levels. As you probably understand, it is important to take care of your vagus nerve, so it can do its job. You'll soon learn how.

JEDI MIND TRICKS

Imagine a car with two adults, three children, a dog, and the stereo at full volume. It will probably be difficult to hear the GPS's voice commands in the car. Life is the same. You are at work for an entire day, making decisions. You come home and take care of your household chores, and family. When everything is done, and you have some time for yourself, everything is still rushing in the nervous system, and you cannot find your GPS. You cannot sort, focus, or be creative because the nervous system is still full of impressions.

Clarity is the ability to listen to your inner wisdom, which is the basis of a good GPS. It's a skill you practice. You gain clarity by creating space for it. There is a direct link between what state your body is in and your ability to hear and act based on your inner wisdom.

There is much you can do to stimulate the vagus nerve and the parasympathetic nervous system. When you stimulate the vagus nerve it creates an inner calm. You feel centered and your inner GPS is heard more clearly. You will now learn #mindhacks that are scientifically proven to stimulate the vagus nerve and activate the parasympathetic nervous system. While these #mindhacks seem simple, don't underestimate the effect of them. They make you land in your body, your system starts to work better, and you create space to connect with your clarity. Feel free to try all the activities and then select at least one that you do daily.

HACK #31

TAKE CARE OF YOUR VAGUS NERVE

DETOX. Pause regularly from TV, news, and social media. Maybe every day after a certain time, half a day, one day a week . . . whatever works for you. What can you do instead of sitting in front of a screen?

FOREST BATHING. One phenomenon that is growing in popularity is *Shin-rin-Yoku*, or "forest bathing." *Shinrin-Yoku* is a Japanese term meaning, "to take in the forest atmosphere with all the senses," which helps people experience nature in a new way and become more present. Several studies show that visits in nature and fresh air reduce the stress hormone cortisol in the body, priming us, and helping our bodies feel good. Therefore, take a walk in the forest. Walk in silence—preferably alone or have your dog accompany you.

MICROPAUSE. After interviews with almost 200 billionaires, icons, and world-class entrepreneurs, author Tim Ferris gathered all the tools these people used to become successful. The result was the book *Tools of Titans*. Guess what at least 80 percent of them did daily? They meditated or did some kind of mindfulness exercise. Being able to direct your awareness to the present is an important skill, as we are constantly processing information. Relaxing and being present in the moment is beneficial. A micropause is a great way to change your state of mind here and now and can give you clarity. I often take a shower when I've too much on my mind. After a few minutes, I feel more present, and it is often there in the shower that my clarity becomes most apparent. Suddenly, I just know what to do. Try to find out what makes you calm, centered, and clear-sighted.

Another good micropause is to be quiet for twenty minutes. It doesn't matter if you sit quietly, meditate, write down what you are grateful for, or stretch. Just be totally present in the moment, and avoid doing anything else at the same time.

BREATHE. Taking five to ten deep and slow breaths does wonders for the nervous system. Deep breathing stimulates the vagus nerve, and it begins to slow down the stress response. My favorite method is called boxing breathing. Breathe in while counting to five. Hold your breath and count to five. Exhale while counting to five. Hold your breath and count to five. Repeat the routine five times.

GET ACTIVATED. Exercise stimulates the vagus nerve. In addition, it is a great way to clear the brain. It will take about ten minutes, but make sure to get your pulse racing during that time.

HOT BATH. Hot water stimulates the vagus nerve and increases blood circulation, which in turn balances the nervous system. Pour some bath salt in the tub, turn off your cellphone, and enjoy. You may even come up with new ideas while in there.

20 COLD, 10 HOT. A while ago I did ice baths and hiked together with Wim Hof, "the Iceman"—an exciting and original man. After his wife's tragic suicide, leaving Wim alone with four children, he fell into a deep depression. Wim explored how he could strengthen his mindset to get over his depression. He realized that if he learned to master his body in the cold, he could also master his mind in other areas of life. Today, he is world famous for his cold baths and breathing exercises, which train the body and the mind to cope with challenges. He has twenty-six world records, including being immersed in icy water for almost two hours. Wim has tested all of the limits of the cold, and many researchers are following him with great interest. Today, he collaborates with several of them to find solutions for the epidemic of mental illness. The best thing about Wim Hof is his attitude: "What I do, anybody can do."

I expose myself to coldness on a slightly smaller scale than Wim Hof. Every morning, I shower alternately hot and cold for five minutes. I start with my butt, then one leg, followed by one arm, and finally the sensitive chest area. Today, I love my cold morning showers. They stimulate my vagus nerve and help me perform better throughout the day. I alternate twenty seconds of cold, followed by ten seconds of warm. I repeat this for ten rounds, a total of five minutes. Start with five seconds cold and ten seconds warm, and gradually increase the time with cold water. The cold water doesn't have to be ice cold; it is enough that it feels really cold.

Cold showers have a number of advantages:

- A stronger immune system
- Less inflammation
- Improved mood

- Mental strength
- You get a more resistant body that can handle strain better
- You wake up faster in the morning and feel healthier
- You can handle stress better
- Lower blood sugar
- Less cravings for unhealthy food
- Better adrenal function
- Better thyroid function
- Better sleep quality
- Increased pain tolerance
- Increased fat-burning capacity
- Increased motivation

HAVE FUN. Spending time with someone you love stimulates the parasympathetic nervous system. Have a cup of coffee or just hang out with someone you can be yourself with. You shouldn't talk about your worries during this time; you should just have fun. Of course, you can also do something fun yourself—something that really gets you in a good mood and makes time fly.

O⊤ HACK #32

END YOUR CLIFF-HANGERS

According to the "Zeigarnik Effect," we are more likely to remember tasks we haven't completed than tasks we have completed. The brain has a strong need to complete what it has begun. When the brain is not allowed to close the loop, it gets stuck. Intrusive thoughts emerge as a way of reminding the cognitive system that something still needs to be completed. We feel good about finishing tasks. The Zeigarnik Effect can also explain why we regret things we didn't do much more than the stuff we've done. Or when we grieve, we seem to focus more on things we didn't say to the person or do with them than what we did experience with them.

TV producers understood this concept and created so-called cliff-hangers. They interrupt the shows when they are at their most exciting points and allow us to wait and wonder a whole week before the next episode. Our brain wants to end the story.

Finish something—be it a task, a relationship, an old sourdough, a habit, or a symbolic ending. Closure gives you peace of mind.

O⎯ⲧ HACK #33

BABY STEPS

One question that often arises in connection with my clients is: "I can hear my GPS, but should I trust it?" The reason you don't trust your internal GPS is often because you haven't used it that often. You don't have much concrete evidence that it is correct. But you will gradually learn that your inner GPS can always be trusted. Exercise in small steps around everyday things. Listen inwardly to what feels right to you, and make small decisions. What do I want to eat? Which movie do I want to see? Should I go to the party? Does this person give me energy?

Gradually, increase the difficulty level. In addition, all of the above #mind-hacks strengthen your signal system, which means that you hear the signals more clearly and can start to interpret the messages; then trust usually comes.

As we begin to follow our gut feelings, we may become fearful of the consequences. What happens if I follow my gut feeling? You might be thinking that you must first build up your courage. Use the 5-Second Rule you learned in Chapter 4 and get started. You can't wait for your courage. Courage is built up through action. 5-4-3-2-1-GO!

In the beginning, it can be tricky to feel the difference between, for example, fear and a healthy sign to back away from a situation or a person. Everyone has their own signals, and it is only you who can decide what is fear or clarity. You will feel the difference soon enough. I feel a calm, safe, steady feeling or a feeling of excitement when my GPS signals what is right. When I'm scared, I feel a fluttering and uneasy feeling in my body.

It is also good to know that what has worked for you before in life may not work now. If you get confused that something you have liked before doesn't feel right anymore, you need to try new things. That's how life works. It might be good to ask yourself, *Am I looking for a distraction so I don't have to look at the real problem or doing the job to be happy? Or do I want to change because it gives me energy and calls me?*

In the beginning, it takes time to find your internal GPS. One trick when you don't feel confident with knowing is to say, "I'll sleep on it" or "Let me think about it over the weekend." Time allows you to let things settle.

O⎯ HACK #34

SIXTY-SECOND DECISIONS

A great way to train your inner clarity is to learn how to make sixty-second decisions. Too much thinking and decision anxiety can cause you to never leave the starting block. Making a sixty-second decision helps you move forward faster and start to trust your gut feeling.

If you have a decision that can be made here and now, give yourself sixty seconds to decide. Try to access all data. When you don't have all the data, trust your gut feeling and personal experience. Delaying decision-making usually doesn't help. Many of the most successful CEOs in the world tend to have a high tolerance for ambiguity. In other words, they can act even though they don't have all the facts on the table or when they face conflicting information. It is a good trait to have because once you have gathered all the facts to make your decision, the opportunity may be gone.

Make a list of decisions you need to make and set your clock.

O⎯ HACK #35

HAVE A BACKUP PLAN

Once you have clarified what excuses you are using for not changing, you can create a backup plan. It is rarely a good idea to come up with a solution in the moment, as it is not usually the best option. However, if you have a backup plan, you can apply it directly and chances are you will choose a better alternative.

The backup plan means that you create a list called IF/THEN, which you use when you have an excuse for not moving forward and following your GPS. You can use the formula when you feel tired, uneasy, stressed, or overwhelmed by everything you need to do—or when you're simply not ready for the next step. Have the list easily accessible so you know what to do when your excuses pop up.

Examples

- IF I feel I have a lack of energy, THEN I walk for five minutes.
- IF I don't want to clean, THEN I'll pick one thing away.
- IF I don't feel that I have time, THEN I'll book time in my calendar to do what I need to do.
- IF I feel overwhelmed by a task, THEN I'll do a small part of it right away.
- IF I don't think I am able or ready, THEN I will count 5-4-3-2-1-GO and do it anyway.

CHAPTER 9 IN 60 SECONDS

- Your internal GPS constantly gives you information about what your route ahead should look like for you to grow and feel good.
- Nothing is wrong when you feel bored, stagnated, frozen, or lost. It is a signal for you need to change something.
- Curiosity and energy are also signals. Your GPS says something is good for you, and you should do more of it.
- Clarity, understanding your GPS, is a skill that is trained.
- **Take care of your vagus nerve.**
  - Detox regularly from TV, news, and social media.
  - Forest bathing in nature. Walk in silence, preferably alone.
  - Micropause and be present for twenty minutes.
  - Take five to ten deep and calming breaths.
  - Get activated. A ten-minute session is enough.
  - Take a warm bath to balance the nervous system.
  - Shower for twenty seconds on cold and ten seconds on warm. Ten rounds, a total of five minutes.
  - Have fun and hang out with someone you like.
- **End your cliff-hangers.** The brain has a tendency to constantly remind you of what you should have done. Get closure.
- **Baby steps.** Listen inwardly and make small decisions. Increase the difficulty level gradually.
- **Sixty-second decisions**. If you have a decision that can be made here and now, give yourself sixty seconds to decide. Trust your gut feeling.
- **Have a backup plan.** Create a list of solutions that help you choose a better alternative instead of doing nothing at all. Always have the list ready.

FOLLOW THE ENERGY

Passion is not a person, place, thing, or goal.
It is an inner state. It's your energy.
You can find your passion by following your energy and curiosity.

When the outside world no longer stimulates us, we feel bored. We buy a new car, find a new partner, or redecorate our home in an attempt to experience something new. When the pleasures of the novelty diminish, we remain on the same route. We long for something more. It is often here that many begin to think about their passions and purpose in life. The soul needs to embark on adventure.

THE GREAT PASSION

I remember the first time I was asked, "What do you want to do in life?" I completely froze. Often, we have never, or at least very rarely, reflected on what we really want to do in life. What would be an adventure for us? What is our passion? We are so busy dealing with all of the practicalities of life that there is no time to think about that question. In addition, it may feel impossible to answer. At least it was for me.

The problem is that we often think too big. We think of the great passion. The one who will give us meaning and joy in life. If we simplify instead, it becomes more tangible and actually something we can start to act on directly:

- Passion is not a destination. Passion is not a person, place, thing, or goal. It is an inner state. It's your energy. It is the feeling of being expanded by something, feeling the scent of possibilities, being excited and happy, and constantly thinking about something. All of these feelings and states are your inner guide, which points you in the right direction.

- You don't need to know what you want to start moving forward. Many of us believe we must find our passion first. Before I started working as a coach, I was looking for my passion and what I wanted to do with my life. I thought and thought and thought and was very frustrated that I didn't realize what I was passionate about. We believe we should suddenly have a magical revelation about what we are meant to do in life, which is completely inaccurate. Passion is something we develop and build. It starts with curiosity, an interest. In the process of developing and getting better, you will discover if the interest turns to love and ultimately to passion—a driving force that makes you disciplined, helps you endure setbacks, and something you want to make sacrifices for.

- Stop thinking that your passion is worthless unless it pays your bills. Your passion can be something that is just for you, and you don't have to earn a penny from it.

REPLACE THE WORD PASSION

What happens if you change the word passion to energy? Ask yourself, "When do I feel energized?" There are certainly activities, people, and situations that will give you energy. If you are looking for what gives you energy, if you follow your curiosity, it can lead you to your passion.

Following your inner GPS, as you learned in Chapter 9, helps you find the direction and what gives you energy. Clarity of what you want will often come when you start moving. You zigzag your way forward and discover along the way what you want and don't want. It is not always possible to calculate everything in advance.

YOU DON'T NEED TO FIND THE RIGHT ONE

We often think in terms of ONE passion, much like *the* right partner, *the* only one, or *the* great love of your life. If you exchange the word passion for energy, you will notice there may be several things that give you energy—even smaller things. You take away the stress of finding only one great passion.

YOU DON'T HAVE TO KNOW HOW

Most often, we think too much about *how* to realize our passion. First and foremost, you need to make a decision. You don't need to know how to do it. For example, if you are considering whether to stay at a job or not, you can start by making the decision. After that, you can think about when is the most responsible time to quit and how to proceed. Start by making the decision. The brain gets stressed when you don't decide. Thinking back and forth drains your energy. Once you have made the decision, let the rest take time until you know how to do it and when to get started.

Follow your energy, feel which decision gives you energy, and say yes to it. If the decision is draining your energy, it is a no. When you find something that gives you energy, do more of it. Even if you don't know how to do it, know you will find your "how" along the way. When you follow the energy, you will find what you like and what gives you joy. When you create energy, you will also get more energy to replace things that don't suit you. It is difficult to grow if, at the same time, you feel exhausted. Therefore, start with the foundation—creating energy. Try things and you will find clues that will help you move forward. You just need to take one step at a time. Remember to build with your Lego pieces, one at a time, as you learned in Chapter 6. Even if you take a wrong turn, it will still give you valuable information. The problem is rarely that you don't know but that you stand still and think instead of try something practical.

A variation of energy is curiosity. I am more driven by curiosity and opportunities than by goals. It's not the goals that make me move forward. As I wrote in Chapter 6, goals are often a thought structure around what we want to achieve. But is that really what we want? We may have an idea that a certain goal will make us happy, but once we reach it, it's not as we thought it would be. Instead, it is often the feeling the goal gives us that we want. We can create these emotions in a variety of other ways. When we are fixed on a specific goal, the risk is that we become blind to other opportunities that may be even better and would give us more satisfaction. This doesn't mean we should not set any goals, but perhaps, we should be more flexible about them. If there is a specific feeling you are looking for, can you create it another way?

Practical goals—for example, to walk a specific number of steps every day or get up at a certain time each morning to catch up with your morning rituals—are good. They give you a reference point to make sure you follow your plan. When it comes to visionary goals, such as growing and developing, where you don't know exactly where you are going, it may be better to follow your energy and curiosity. It is often so much more fun and inspiring than setting goals.

Personally, I have changed my formula from passion, goals, and purpose to energy, curiosity, and opportunities. It helps me enjoy the journey more. I don't suspend my happiness and satisfaction around the finish line, and I don't feel unsuccessful if I don't reach the goal. Often, I find an exciting turn-off road, and if I follow it, something even better shows up afterward. And don't forget that if you get stuck, become bored, feel exhausted, experience powerlessness or loss, it doesn't mean something is wrong; it's just time to move forward.

YOU DON'T NEED TO TAKE THE STRAIGHT PATH

I like the author Elizabeth Gilbert's story about jackhammers and hummingbirds. She describes two types of people. Jackhammers have a super focus on the target and hammer through everything until they reach their destination. They are efficient and get things done but have a tendency to become obsessed, stubborn, and loud.

Hummingbirds fly from tree to tree, flower to flower, and taste a bit here and a bit there. They create a rich life for themselves, and they cross-pollinate the world. They take an idea with them to the next place, where they learn something else. They then weave together everything they have learned and open up to something new. If you continue to follow your path, you will one day discover that you are exactly in the right place. You are with the right people, in the right city, or in the right project. If you follow your curiosity, it will lead you to your passion. If you don't take the straight path to your goals, it can actually be an advantage.

🖤 YODA MOMENT

Be honest with yourself about what you want to achieve. When setting a goal or curiously investigating something, ask yourself, *Is this a priority? Am I ready to make a change? Am I willing to do what it takes?* For example, if you want to lose weight, are you willing to change your diet and exercise? If you want to start your own business, are you willing to earn less the first few years and devote much of your time to getting the company on its feet? Be completely honest when defining your priorities. If something is important to you, you will find the time, energy, and opportunities. If it is not a priority, stop spending time and energy, and drop it. Choose something that gives you energy, something you want to strive for. Distinguish between the fear of not daring to change and a lack of will to change.

- What in your life do you want to change?
- What do you want to learn?
- What gives you energy?
- What are you curious about?
- What are you willing to do to succeed?
- What in your life is not a priority and something you can let go of?

Now break down your goal into small Lego pieces. What is the first Lego piece you can put in place? Think small and change one thing at a time. Explore. Follow the energy and your curiosity.

⚙ JEDI MIND TRICKS

Don't look for your passion outside of yourself. Instead, unlock the energy already inside you. You don't need all the answers from the start.

🔑 HACK #36

OPEN MORE DOORS

Notice people, situations and activities that make you feel energized. It can be a feeling of ease, joy, or that you've expanded and see more opportunities. One step may also be to identify what you don't want. Notice if you feel tired, drained, powerless, heavy, stuck, or bored.

The exploration itself is exciting, just like an adventure. Allow yourself to explore different interests, topics, and areas to see what feels right. To over-think is a trap. It's easy to believe that just because you are thinking about your future, you have control and are on your way toward your goals. Stop thinking and start exploring. Follow your heart. You don't have to make big leaps. Place one Lego piece at a time. And regardless of the results, you will grow and learn new things.

See if you can stop using the sentence "I need this to . . ." *I need to change my job to feel inspired. I need to find a partner to be happy. I need to lose ten kilograms to be happy with myself. I need a bigger house to feel successful.* When we want a specific result—"If I do this, then this should happen"—and it doesn't happen, we often become upset, disappointed, and sad. When we take away what we think we need to be happy and release the idea that just one result counts, new doors will open for us to feel good. It can be anything that makes us happy, satisfied, safe, calm, or energized. It doesn't have to be the job, the partner, losing the weight, or the new house.

If there is something special you like doing, set aside time for it. Don't analyze. Who says you have to make money from what you like to do? It's totally okay to have a regular job and do something you enjoy on the side. No jobs are perfect, even if the job in question is your passion. You will not always fly out of bed in the morning just because you have a passion.

Are you a person who must constantly see the benefits in everything you do? Exercise must not only be fun; it must also be effective. *If you can't make a living from your hobby, it is not worth doing it* is a lie. There is a great benefit in "just" feeling the joy. It gives you energy that makes you a happier person and a better parent, partner, friend, and fellow human being.

⊙┰ HACK #37

SUCCESS FORMULA

Even if you know what gives you energy or what your passion is, it's not enough to succeed. Hard work alone doesn't always lead to success. The most scientific psychometric personality test, The Hexaco, states there are four facets that affect your success. Hard work is only 25 percent of the formula; three additional components are required:

- **25 percent hard work.** How hard are you willing to work to get where you want? If you cannot spend the time required by the task, you need to change the goal or timeline. If you don't want to put in the hours, drop the idea.
- **25 percent perfectionism.** You don't have to be a perfectionist all of the time or in all areas. But when something is important to you, you need to double-check and make sure everything is in tip-top order.
- **25 percent organization.** Take ten minutes each morning and organize your day so you stay focused and prioritize correctly.
- **25 percent good judgment.** The ability to make the right decisions is important. You need your clarity and your GPS. If you do the other three components correctly but lack the ability to make the right decisions, it will take longer to reach your goal. In Chapter 9 you received tips about how to activate your internal GPS. Follow your gut feeling, learn from people who are where you want to be, and use all of the free resources available on the Internet.

o—π HACK #38

A FEEL-GOOD LIST

When we don't know who we are, what we want, what we like, or what makes us happy and gives us energy, it is easy for us to "borrow" goals from the rest of society: money, a partner, a new job, a new house, or a vacation. We believe we will be happy when we achieve these goals because it seemed to work for others. Instead of borrowing the stereotypical goals, use your imagination. Make your own list of what makes you feel happy. They can be small, simple things.

I know I'm successful/happy/feel good when:

- I have a free afternoon.
- My daily to-do list contains no more than three things.
- I have meditated in the morning.
- I work out two times per week.

- I can read bedtime stories to my children in peace.

O⟶ HACK #39

ENGAGE IN "MISSION 90"

How do you experience the energy in the areas listed below in your life? What do you want to do more or less of? What do you need to do to change the energy in each area?

- Health (body and mind)
- Love and connection (family and friends)
- Having fun (leisure and hobbies)
- Work (career and financial position)
- Spirituality (soul, growing and contributing)

What do you want to achieve in the next ninety days? What are you curious about? What is most important to you right now? Choose *one* area and *one* step that would make the biggest positive difference in your life. Be specific. For example, saying, "I should try to be healthier" doesn't work. Trying is just a wish. What is *one* thing you can do every day to become healthier?

You need to prioritize *one* area, *one* goal or vision, and *one* step. It can be difficult to have too many goals, working on several areas, and accomplish a large number of actions at the same time. It's much like renovating an entire house at the same time. You start fixing something in every room, but nothing ever gets finished. When you multitask, you are less effective, and that also applies to goals and visions.

Give your ninety-day project a theme that summarizes your commitment to your mission and reminds you of what it is you want to achieve. Feel free to visualize every morning how you do your actions, how it feels, how proud you are of yourself, and how you will feel after your ninety days.

Why Exactly Ninety Days?

We tend to forget goals that are too far away, or we lose momentum if the distance is too long. Or we think we have plenty of time and postpone what needs to be done. That is why one-year goals are sometimes difficult to reach. When it comes to short-term goals, we often overestimate what we can accomplish in a month. As everyday life sneaks up on us, we lose focus and drive. Ninety days is a reasonable period of time.

Extra Tips to Succeed With Your "Mission 90"

Your focus and energy level are usually best in the morning. For ninety days, can you spend some time in the morning to get to where you want?

CHAPTER 10 IN 60 SECONDS

- Passion is not something you spontaneously find or think yourself toward; it is something you develop.
- Passion is energy. Follow your energy and curiosity.
- Ask the right question. When do I feel energized? Identify what you want to do more of. Do less of what drains your energy.
- You don't need all of the answers from the start.
- **Open more doors.** Exploring is exciting, like an adventure. Discover along the way what feels right.
- **The success formula.** [25 percent hard work. 25 percent perfectionism. 25 percent organization. 25 percent good judgment.]
- **Feel-good-list.** Don't borrow others' goals. Make your own list of what makes you feel happy.
- **Mission 90.** What do you want to accomplish in the next ninety days? Choose *one* area, *one* goal/vision, and *one* step that you think would make the biggest positive difference in your life.

THE INTELLIGENCE OF THE HEART

Your heart acts like a brain and helps you reach a deeper form of intelligence.
In the heart you can connect with the extraordinary within you.

The heart is our home. This is where love and magic live. This is where you were all the time, when you were a kid. Here, everything is possible. Here, you can manifest everything you want to achieve in life. This is where miracles happen. The heart should have its own book, but I would like to give you just a taste of its intelligence.

In today's society, we ascribe great importance to the brain. For many, the heart is just a pumping mechanism responsible for transporting blood to our organs. But the heart is so much more. In 1991, researchers discovered about 40,000 specialized cells in the heart, called sensory neurites, which are exactly the same as our brain cells. These cells think, remember, and make decisions independently. The heart can learn through experience and act completely independent of the brain.

The heart generates the strongest electromagnetic field of all the organs; and therefore, affects everything in our body. The heart's magnetic component is 5,000 times stronger than the brain's magnetic field and can be read several meters from the body with a sensitive magnetometer. There are many more fibers that run from the heart to the brain than the other way around. We get tons of information from our heart. The brain and the heart are interconnected through the vagus nerve, and many of the instructions the brain gets are actually from the heart.

According to neuro-cardiologists and researchers, the heart functions as a brain, helping us with a deeper form of intelligence. If we can connect our brains and hearts and use the intelligence of both, we open the door to the extraordinary—or the mysterious—which monks and shamans are alleged to experience. We are actually coded to have these experiences in our everyday lives. By using our hearts, we can, among other things, gain access to our intuition, contact our subconscious, get a sense of the future, and increase our pace of learning. In the West, we are so used to living up in our heads and in our brains that we sometimes have trouble getting in touch with our hearts. But what if we could get in touch with the intelligence of the heart?

THE HEART - THE FIFTH BRAIN

The heart starts beating twenty-two days after conception and is the first organ to be formed in the fetus. The heart has its own independent complex nervous system called the "brain of the heart." Thus, the heart has its own intelligence and neuro-cardiologists often call the heart the fifth brain. This is about the evolution of our brain where we have previously recognized four brains: the reptile brain, limbic system (mammalian brain), neocortex, and prefrontal cortex. And now the heart. The fifth brain, which is in the heart, is believed to have the ability to develop the power to transcend. Transcending means going beyond the physical, beyond the ego. Here we have the ability to get to know and be ourselves.

GET TO KNOW YOUR HEART

In our daily lives, our attention is usually directed outward rather than inward. All day long, we are in a chain of thoughts and experiences; we rarely take the time to just be with ourselves. Therefore, we rarely get to know ourselves on a deeper level.

If you regularly meditate with focus on the heart, you will get to know yourself and become yourself—who you really are. Think of your heart as a very close friend who only has your best interests at heart. The heart always takes you back to your center, and this is where you can connect with the extraordinary inside of you.

YODA MOMENT

- When do you feel you are connected with your heart?
- If you have no contact with your heart, what has happened that has caused you to lose the connection?
- What could you do to reconnect with your heart?

JEDI MIND TRICKS

When we focus on the heart, it is said we are in contact with every part of the Universe, and we have access to the universal field of intelligence. Dr. Leonard Laskow, who has been studying the healing power of love for thirty-three years, believes the heart is the source of all healing. He has even proven that the love of the heart can reduce the growth of tumors by more than 30 percent.

If you want more information about the importance of the heart for your growth, I recommend you visit the HeartMath Institute. Since 1991, they have researched and developed scientifically proven tools to help people build a bridge between the heart and the brain.

O━ HACK #40

PRACTICE HEART MEDITATION

With the following method from best-selling author Gregg Braden, you can get in touch with your heart and use its intelligence and power.

1. Sit comfortably and close your eyes. Switch your focus from your external to your internal world. Closing the eyes sends a signal to the body to turn inward.

2. Focus on your heart and heart chakra. This shows the heart that you want to connect. One hint is to touch your heart, maybe by placing the palm of your hand against your chest, as you do in some cultures when you greet someone. Or as the Buddhists do, allowing the palms to meet in

front of the chest while the thumbs touch the heart chakra or by lightly touching the heart chakra with your finger. Your heart chakra is located in the center of the chest (at the sternum), a little above the heart. When you physically touch your heart area, your awareness and focus will be directed there.

3. Slow down your breathing. This sends a signal to the body that you are safe, as breathing only slows down when you feel secure. This safe signal alters the body chemistry, calms down the nervous system, and silences the brain. As you breathe, imagine that the breath comes from the heart.

4. Develop one of the following feelings: love, appreciation, gratitude, thoughtfulness, or compassion. These emotions activate the energy of the heart, which is chemically reflected in the body and causes it to relax and feel good. We also connect the heart network with the brain.

5. Sit for a moment and rest in the feeling you chose. If you don't have a question that you want answered, you can finish here. If you have a question, continue with item #6.

6. Ask a question to your heart, something you need to know. Your heart knows. The question should be brief and precise. The heart doesn't need a long drawn out explanation. The heart speaks clearly and directly. If not, redo the process, and let the body know that you are seeking the intelligence of the heart and not the egos.

Everyone experiences their heart meditation differently. You can feel butterflies in your stomach, a warm feeling around your body, or a tingling in your fingertips. You may not feel any physical sensations at all, only thoughts. Or you may experience both. If you don't experience much in the beginning, keep practicing.

Heart Meditation and "The Zone"

You may remember the gamma brain waves you learned about in Chapter 8. These are associated with laser focus, high mental and physical ability, and feelings of happiness. When you meditate—and especially if you focus on the heart and a sense of gratitude, compassion, and love—gamma waves increase. People with high levels of gamma activity are exceptionally intelligent, have great compassion, and exhibit strong self-control.

The benefits of producing more gamma brain waves are that you more often feel as if you are in "The Zone." Everything flows. You feel happier, calmer, and more satisfied. Your experiences become richer, you have a sharper focus, your brain can process more information faster, and you increase your creativity, memory capacity, and self-control.

CHAPTER 11 IN 60 SECONDS

- Your heart acts like a brain and helps you reach a deeper form of intelligence.
- The brain and heart are connected through the vagus nerve. It is important that you activate it. See Chapter 9.
- When you use your heart, you can tap into superpowers, such as stronger intuition, quick learning, contact with your subconscious, and a sense of the future.
- The "fifth brain," which is in the heart, is believed to have the ability to go beyond the physical, where you have the ability to know and be yourself.
- When you meditate with focus on the heart, you activate gamma brain waves. These will help you into "The Zone"—when everything flows.
- **Heart Meditation.** Get to know your heart. Do the meditation in this chapter to connect the heart's network with the brain.

YOU ARE THE ONE

You are not The One because you are chosen.
You are The One because you choose to be.

Movie scene: Dark skyscrapers rising toward the sky. The rain is pouring down. Lightning splits the sky. Like a meteor, Agent Smith plunges Neo down from the sky and onto the ground. The impact creates a huge crater, with Neo lying in the mud.

Agent Smith: Why, Mr. Anderson? Why, why, why? Why do you do it? Why? Why get up? Why keep fighting? Do you believe you're fighting for something? For more than your survival? Can you tell me what it is? Do you even know?

Neo laboriously rises from the ground.

Agent Smith: Why, Mr. Anderson? Why do you persist?!

Neo: Because I choose to.

(From the movie, *The Matrix Revolutions*, 2003) [7]

7   Lana and Lilly Wachowski, dirs. *The Matrix Revolutions*. Burbank, CA: Village Roadshow Pictures, 2003.

Neo highlights the biggest asset we have here on Earth: our free will. That's the answer to the question of how to get out of *The Matrix*. Your own active choice to become a rebel to own your POWER and FREEDOM. To do the right thing with determination. Both to yourself and others.

You are the One.
Make it happen.
It shall be!

Karin

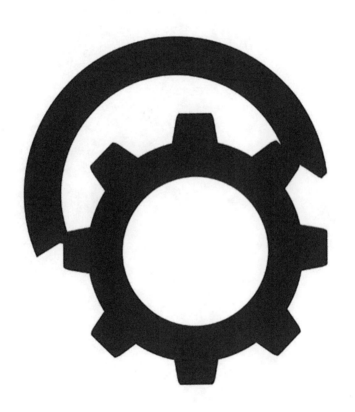

INDEX OF THE JEDI MIND TRICKS

#1 Crush the ANTs
Say STOP and replace your automatic negative thoughts with positive, constructive, and realistic anchor thoughts, which you have prepared in advance.

#2 Visualize like a Navy Seal
Visualize for thirty to sixty seconds each morning, steering your thoughts and emotions toward a positive and active state.

#3 Create A Winning Morning
Establish morning rituals to help you create a successful day. No phones in the bedroom and no snooze-button in the morning.

#4 Boost your willpower
Avoid decision fatigue and impulsive actions by creating routines and taking breaks during the day.

#5 Collect Gold Nuggets
Collect what has been good during the day. Close your eyes, make the experience vivid and "snuggle" for twenty to thirty seconds.

#6 The 5-Second Rule

When you have an instinct to act toward a goal or when you hesitate, count 5-4-3-2-1-GO. Let go of the brake and move.

#7 Stop Complaining

To complain isn't to observe what is happening, it's a choice to zoom in on the bad things. Complaining reinforces your negative default mode.

#8 Follow Your Code of Honor

Following your moral code is important to feeling proud of yourself. Pride strengthens your self-esteem.

#9 Be Generous with Praise

Praise yourself for who you are and for your efforts. The most important praise is your own. Other's praise is the icing on the cake.

#10 Leave the Middle Line

Focus on your strengths and do more of what you're good at.

#11 Become Friends with the Emotions

Examine your feelings. When you understand them, they become less scary.

#12 Hit the Pause Button

After ninety seconds of an emotional storm, you can choose whether or not to stay in the emotional loop.

#13 The Five-Minute Trick

When something goes wrong, allow yourself to fully experience all of your feelings for five minutes. After five minutes, start looking ahead. What can be done?

#14 Change the Label

Replace a negative label with something reinforcing and positive, such as an anchor thought.

#15 Slow Down

To gain control over your fear, slow down. Your brain will work better, and you can break down your problem into smaller parts.

#16 Dare to and You Will Win

Train your body's response by facing what you are afraid of. Choose one thing you stopped yourself from doing because of fear, and do it!

#17 Replace Your Strategies

Make a list of the strategies you use today when you are scared and which strategies you intend to use instead.

#18 Build with Legos

Big goals can make you overwhelmed. Break down your goals into tiny Lego pieces. Focus on building and exploring. See where the building is leading you.

#19 List Your Favorite Excuses

The things you don't do . . . are they really a priority for you? Reassess and focus on what is important to you.

#20 Own Your Success

You can be both happy where you are today and strive forward at the same time. Write down what you are content with in your life.

#21 Cultivate a Growth Mindset

Take on the challenges, learn more, and appreciate the lessons. See and praise your efforts. And do the work. Devotion trumps talent.

#22 Hello Friend!

Get to know every part of yourself and let each part take its place. What are your different parts trying to do for you? All parts are important, and everyone is needed in the team.

#23 Guilt Sanitation

Deal with people and situations where you should have acted differently. Forgive yourself for the mistakes you have made.

#24 Stay in Touch

Get in touch with family, friends, and acquaintances. Say yes to their invitations.

#25 Create Your Power Mantra

Create a mantra that contains action and becomes your beacon to keep you on the right track.

#26 Dare to Receive

All positive actions aimed at you are signs of love. Open the door to your heart and dare to receive.

#27 Unwind

Learn self-hypnosis to unwind to a state of slower brain waves, so your system works better.

#28 Make a Brain Dump

Write down everything you are worried about not catching up with or managing and everything you need to do. Draw a circle around the most important thing you need to do for something concrete to happen, and do it first.

#29 Become an Explorer

Explore who you are and what you want to change in your life by opening the door to your subconscious where all your programs are.

#30 Edit Your Story

What is your story, or excuse, for not being where you want in life? Decide to edit your story.

#31 Take Care of Your Vagus Nerve

- Detox regularly from TV, news, and social media.
- Forest bathe in nature. Walk in silence, preferably alone.
- Micropause and be present for twenty minutes.
- Take five to ten deep and calming breaths.
- Get activated. A ten-minute session is enough.
- Take a warm bath to balance the nervous system.
- Shower twenty seconds cold and ten seconds hot, ten rounds, a total of five minutes.
- Have fun and hang out with someone you like.

#32 End Your Cliff-Hangers

The brain has a tendency to constantly remind you of what you should have done. Get closure.

#33 Take Baby Steps

Listen inward and make small decisions. Increase the difficulty level gradually.

#34 Make Sixty-Second Decisions

If you have a decision that can be made here and now, give yourself sixty seconds to decide. Trust your gut feeling.

#35 Have a Backup Plan

Create a list of solutions that help you choose a better alternative instead of doing nothing at all. Always have the list ready.

#36 Open More Doors

Exploring is exciting, like an adventure. Discover along the way what feels right.

#37 Use the Success Formula
- 25 percent hard work
- 25 percent perfectionism
- 25 percent organization
- 25 percent good judgment

#38 Create a Feel-Good List
Don't borrow other people's goals. Make your own list of what makes you feel happy.

#39 Engage in "Mission 90"
What do you want to accomplish in the next ninety days? Choose ONE area, ONE goal/vision, and ONE step that you think would make the biggest positive difference in your life.

#40 Practice Heart Meditation
Get to know your heart. Do the meditation in this chapter to connect the heart's network with the brain.

FOR FURTHER READING

Books for the curious one:

- *Breaking the Habit of Being Yourself: How to Lose Your Mind and Create a New One* by Dr. Joe Dispenza
- The Biology of Belief: Unleashing the Power of Consciousness, Matter and Miracles by Bruce H Lipton
- *The Inside-Out Revolution: The Only Thing You Need to Know to Change Your Life Forever* by Michael Neill
- *The 5 Second Rule: The Surprisingly Simple Way to Live, Love, and Speak with Courage* by Mel Robbins
- *Mindset: The New Psychology of Success* by Carol S. Dweck
- *Tools of Titans: The Tactics, Routines, and Habits of Billionaires, Icons, and World-Class Performers* by Timothy Ferriss
- *Man's Search for Meaning* by Viktor E. Frankl
- *The Power of Habit* by Charles Duhigg
- The Real Happy Pill by Anders Hansen
- *The Awakened Family: How to Raise Empowered, Resilient, and Conscious Children* by Shefali Tsabary
- *Wired for Love: How Understanding Your Partner's Brain and Attachment Style Can Help You Defuse Conflict and Build a Secure Relationship* by Stan Tatkin
- *Thinking, Fast and Slow* by Daniel Kahneman
- *The Journey Home: Autobiography of an American Swami* by Radhanath Swami

ABOUT THE AUTHOR

Karin Tydén is a mind hacker, multi-award-winning coach, hypnotherapist, and facilitator. She has a Bachelor's Degree in Media and Communications. Karin has worked as a TV producer, marketing director, PR consultant, brand manager, and success manager for more than twenty-five years.

Karin is the winner of the 2019 and 2020 European Enterprise Award, Recognized Leader in Mental Health Training Services, "Life Coach of the Year," and Corporate Innovation & Excellence Awards 2020. Karin has an almost supernatural ability to understand and "hack" the mechanics behind people's subconscious patterns to create new and better strategies in life.

She lives in Sweden but is active in more than twenty-five countries and is one of Europe's sharpest in her field. She has helped thousands of people maximize their potential and is often the coaches' coach. Karin's book *Mind Hacking for Rebels* has been very well received in Sweden, and the book is now finding its way to the rest of the world.

Stay in touch with Karin at www.karintyden.se.

A free ebook edition is available with the purchase of this book.

To claim your free ebook edition:

1. Visit MorganJamesBOGO.com
2. Sign your name CLEARLY in the space
3. Complete the form and submit a photo of the entire copyright page
4. You or your friend can download the ebook to your preferred device

Morgan James BOGO™

A **FREE** ebook edition is available for you or a friend with the purchase of this print book.

CLEARLY SIGN YOUR NAME ABOVE

Instructions to claim your free ebook edition:
1. Visit MorganJamesBOGO.com
2. Sign your name CLEARLY in the space above
3. Complete the form and submit a photo of this entire page
4. You or your friend can download the ebook to your preferred device

Print & Digital Together Forever.

Snap a photo

Free ebook

Read anywhere